THE POWER
OF THE
SECOND
QUESTION

CHRIS SKELLETT trained at the University of Birmingham, England, and has worked for over 30 years as a clinical psychologist. A former national president of the Hospital Psychologists Association, he has also served on the executive boards of the New Zealand Psychology Society and the New Zealand College of Clinical Psychologists.

Chris is a popular workshop presenter and speaker, and is the author of the widely acclaimed book *When Happiness is Not Enough: Balancing pleasure and achievement in your life*. His workshops focus on a) lifestyle balance and b) the development of personal insight and valuing personal wisdom. Workshops can be tailored to specific groups on request and Chris is available to speak internationally.

Chris is married with two adult daughters, having recently lost his son to epilepsy at the age of 21. He lives with his wife on a small rural property in the South Island of New Zealand.

To find out more about Chris and his workshops,
please visit: www.chrisskellettconsulting.co.nz

THE POWER
OF THE
SECOND
QUESTION

Finding simple truths for complex lives

CHRIS SKELLETT
MSc Clin Psych

First published 2014

Exisle Publishing Pty Ltd
'Moonrising', Narone Creek Road, Wollombi, NSW 2325, Australia
P.O. Box 60–490, Titirangi, Auckland 0642, New Zealand
www.exislepublishing.com

A CiP record for this book is available from the National Library of Australia

ISBN 978 1 921966 42 2

Design and typesetting by Christabella Designs
Typeset in Bembo 11/19pt
Printed in Shenzhen, China, by Ink Asia

This book uses paper sourced under ISO 14001 guidelines from well-managed forests and other controlled sources.

10 9 8 7 6 5 4 3 2 1

The author would like to pay special thanks to Judith Beck PhD, for giving permission to disclose the story 'Something interesting always happens when we get lost', that appears on page 61; and to Russ Harris for permission to reference on page 84 questions used in his book *ACT Made Simple: An easy to read primer on Acceptance and Commitment Therapy*, New Harbinger Publications, 2009.

Please note that, where appropriate for reasons of privacy, names have been changed.

DISCLAIMER

For my son, Henry Skellett
2 May 1992–15 May 2013

Someone so true . . .

Henry lived his life as a young man ... in the present moment and in a world of activity, adventure and fun. Not for Henry the vacuous speculation of an older man. His dad was too full of waffle. He took it upon himself to keep me honest and grounded as I wrote this book. It is such a shame that he didn't live long enough to see the finished product. I would have valued his opinion of it above the opinion of all others.

He was truly wise beyond his years.

CONTENTS

Preface

Every so often we come across a simple truth that makes a personal connection for us. It could be a familiar quote or saying. It could be a politician's catch phrase or a family motto. Sometimes it comes naively from the mouth of an innocent child. Or it could be simple advice from a friend. Sometimes it's a comedian's wicked one-liner.

These simple truths capture complex issues in a single phrase; reflecting the world as we see it. It resonates with us.

When this happens, we experience an 'aha' moment. We have gained insight or perhaps experienced a transformational moment. Suddenly we realise something about life that we probably already knew but hadn't fully acknowledged. This is a personal 'light bulb' moment and we become wiser as a result.

Each of us carries a collection of personal 'truths' about our world, our relationships and ourselves. They help us make sense of the business of being alive. They are often derived from our life experience, but they are also handed down to us by the people that we have known or know. They are subjective beliefs that organise the way that we see the world.

But how often do we take the time to reflect and consider the full depth and breadth of our 'personal wisdom'? We are so busy living life in the moment that we rarely make time to pull up and see the bigger picture. Our accumulated experience inevitably makes us wiser as individuals but, generally, we tend not to appreciate how far we have come.

The Power of the Second Question is about creating the opportunity to pause, to reflect and to consider exactly who we are. To affirm what we value in life and what general principles guide our behaviour. It asks us to consider what lessons we have learned as we have travelled life's journey, and what our wise legacy should be. This book is about finding ways to see a bigger picture, to help us to discover the meaning and sense of purpose in our lives.

And how can we see the bigger picture? How can we extract a wiser perspective on our world?

By asking good thought-provoking questions of ourselves, we can pause, take a breath and reflect more expansively about life. We also need to set aside time to encourage this habit.

As we grow older we become wiser naturally. This is because we do less and we think more. This cognitive shift towards reflection becomes increasingly relevant and important to us as we age. As a result, we can see patterns repeating themselves. We listen to the stories of others and we react with a more measured, less emotional response. The specific details of a situation become less important. Instead, we become more interested in distilling the essential message from a story and finding a broader coherence. We become 'detached observers' or commentators on the life that goes on around us. Experience also allows us to become more accepting and philosophical about life.

Knowing a little more about life is about learning to know more about ourselves and our core beliefs. This enables us to live a more authentic life, without feeling constricted by the opinions of others. We become our own person and we carry a more defined personal compass that gives direction to our lives. But this is not an automatic process and it is easy to drift rather aimlessly through life. To reset that compass we sometimes need to ask challenging questions of ourselves; questions that elicit a personal wisdom. These questions are known as 'second questions'. In *The Power of the Second Question* we will learn how to ask them and how to extract greater wisdom from both ourselves and from those around us.

The Power of the Second Question invites you to lift up from the practicalities of everyday life to consider the bigger picture. To think about who you are, what you have learned, and where you are going.

How to use this book

You probably bought this book and intended to keep it clean and pristine. You will try not to mark the pages or bend the spine. Although you will be asked to write in the book and complete exercises you may well hold back, reluctant to spoil the freshness of the book. This is how we usually treat the books we buy.

However, this book isn't like that. It's a book to engage with, to interact with and to scribble in. This is *your book*, and not one to be lightly shared with others. It is the opportunity for you to reflect upon your life, and to pull together key insights about who *you* are, what you stand for, and what you value in this wonderful business of being alive.

This is a workbook. I encourage you to scrawl in it, to jot down insights and thoughtful ideas in the margins. Feel free to dog-ear special pages. To jump around in it and come back to different sections time and time again. Think about the questions that appeal to you or challenge you, making time to reflect on them. The more you batter this book, the richer you will become.

I once counselled a client who worked in a book bindery. As a farewell gift, she gave me a beautifully bound leather book with my name etched in gold lettering down the spine. It was a fantastic gift which I treasured. I initially planned to use my beautifully bound book to write a factual history of my life, one page per year, but the task seemed to be too overwhelmingly complex to know quite where to begin. Somehow the project lacked passion, and it didn't seem to capture the essence of who I was. It may have told others what I'd done in my life, but it wouldn't tell them what I'd learned. Or what I valued. Or what life was all about for me.

My beautiful book, so highly valued, deserved something better. It needed more spark. I realised that I would far prefer to use it to collate my personal insights, my treasured stories, and my favourite quotes into one specific place. I also wanted to add photos, news clippings, and favourite cartoons. In short, I wanted to create a personal statement that captured the essential highlights of my life, my personal learnings and the key ideas that underpinned my world view. The empty pages were to become the blank canvas for my personal reflections, and they would eventually stand as my legacy for others to enjoy.

I suggest that you buy a book of empty pages for yourself. It could be anything from a simple school exercise book to a special leather-bound copy like mine. Either way, get hold of a book that is full of blank pages. Then set aside time to transcribe your insights, your simple truths and your wisdom from *The Power of the Second Question*. Arrange them as you wish. But find ways to capture who you are, what you stand for and what life is all about for you. Pull together all the wise words you have ever heard and all the insights that you have gained. The lyrics of favourite songs, pictures of personal significance, and cartoons that capture an issue perfectly for you. Record the collection of simple truths that speak for you.

It will become *your* book. A book that represents who you truly are.

Introduction

We all live from day to day. We eat, we sleep and we exercise, and then we repeat the pattern all over again. We laugh. We have fun. We get things done. Sometimes, it's good, sometimes it's not so good. But we trudge on regardless, taking each day as it comes.

As our lives unfold, we all know, deep down, that there is something more to life; a deeper, more insightful level of awareness that we never quite seem to have the time to access. Occasionally we might hear an intriguing comment or we suddenly realise something that seems quite profound, but then we push on with the issues of the day, and the transient insight slips quietly away.

How hard is it for us to pause and reflect about what really matters in our lives? We really owe it to ourselves to stop and be more appreciative of the opportunities for insight that life has provided. We need to pause ... and we need to reflect.

Why is this so important? Our individual behaviour is governed largely by unwritten rules about life that we learn along the way. We evolve general truths about how the world seems to operate and we are guided by a set of vaguely articulated personal values. We decide who to trust, and what to believe, and we shape our own definitions of success. We define what constitutes a personally fulfilling life and we generate simple guidelines to help us achieve it.

By doing this we accumulate a personal set of *subjective truths* that underpin the way that we see the world. These truths are the core beliefs that come to define who we are.

Core beliefs are created by taking a rather selective view of how the world functions. When core beliefs clash between people, they are the primary drivers of wars. When they align, they are the fundamental ingredients of love.

Dr Foster's Good Question

Several years ago I was visited by the father of a good friend of mine. He used to be my family doctor when I was a child, but it was a retired, kindly figure in his late eighties who approached me, leaning heavily on a walking stick and cupping one hand behind his ear to hear me speak.

On shaking my hand firmly, he fixed me with a steely eye and asked, 'Chris, what have you been doing since I saw you last?'

'Well,' I replied proudly, 'for the last 25 years I've been working as a clinical psychologist.'

'Good Lord,' he replied, 'And over all that time, *what have you learned about people?*'

I was totally stumped for a reply! The daunting size of the question completely overwhelmed me. In 25 years of clinical practice, I had never stopped to think about this. No one had ever asked me such a question before and I had never stopped to ask the question of myself.

A whole range of useless comments sprang to mind, but essentially I was totally ill-equipped to offer Dr Foster any significant wisdom from my accumulated experience. Despite many years of incredible conversations with a huge range of thoughtful clients, I had never stopped to distil my key insights or to collect my broader thoughts about what I had learned.

Dr Foster's Good Question gave me the initial impetus to write this book. It was the start of a thoughtful, integrative period of my life where I started to value the wisdom of my experience, and to use it as a powerful companion to my knowledge and formal training. I also realised that good therapy is not really about giving wise advice, but instead providing clients with the opportunity to find their own 'simple truths', and to gain fundamental shifts in perspective that help them move forward. In short, my role essentially was to ask them good, thought-provoking questions.

More importantly, I also realised that *we don't need to be in therapy* to reflect usefully upon our lives. For all of us, the habit of asking ourselves good, penetrating questions is an essential part of living life well. *The Power of the Second Question* gives you the opportunity to do just that.

The power of a second question

Let's look more closely at the role of these expansive questions that can elicit profound 'aha' moments. We call them 'second questions' because they usually follow on from a series of factual questions that simply exchange information. Second questions are qualitatively different from the more frequently asked factual questions. They provide an extra dimension to a conversation. They lift us up. They open a door. They are usually big picture, conceptual questions that require the respondent to pause and consider before they reply. They make us think more expansively, often on topics that we haven't previously considered, and they challenge us to declare a personal wisdom.

Practical examples of second questions in action

In therapy

Clinical psychologists, psychotherapists and counsellors are all adept at using good questions to elicit 'aha' moments. They are taught to create 'transformational' insights in their clients in this way.

As a therapist, you know when you've asked a good question in a therapy conversation. There's a thoughtful pause from the client, a moment of reflection, and possibly a deep sigh before they provide a simple, often profound response. The answer often reveals a dramatic and fundamental change in their world view. Once they experience this change, possibilities open up to explore new ways of thinking and of overcoming problems.

Examples of these broad insights might be:

- I'm looking back. I need to look forward.
- I'm not a victim, I'm a survivor.

In therapy, clients learn to reconceptualise their situation in a way that empowers them and leads them forward. A new truth arrives that dramatically transforms their world view. It usually arrives after about half an hour of apparently idle chat and in response to a good question.

In celebrity interviews

We can also see the power of a good question when watching celebrity interviews on television. A film star might be being interviewed about their latest movie. They might be asked about what it's like to live in Hollywood. Or what it's like to work with a certain petulant co-star. And then, almost without fail, the interviewer will ask a powerful second question.

The conversation will seem to shift gear. The interviewer will pause and collect themselves before asking something more 'big picture' or something more abstract. They will ask an overarching question that invites the respondent to share an insight and the question usually elicits a surprising degree of wisdom from the interviewee.

For example, they may ask: 'Overall, what do you think is the key quality of a good actor?'

Again we see the pause, the sigh and the moment of reflection before a simple truth is revealed.

The reply might be that 'It's all about the ability to connect with the audience,' or 'It's all about being authentic, and truly believing in the character.'

It was the power of the second question that drew the wisdom from them.

Different actors will answer the question differently, but at the end of the day, they will each be offering their personal wisdom about the industry. They will be offering a subjective truth that tells us more about them as people. And of greater interest here, we can see that they may not even have been aware of their wisdom until they spoke it.

In the classroom

Good teachers do not simply teach facts; they also ask good questions. Telling children what the three main functions of a river are is both useful and informative, but *asking* them to think about what the three main functions of a river might be will add significantly to the process. By asking good questions, the children are encouraged to think critically, encouraged to 'own' their answers, and also to access internalised wisdom that they perhaps didn't even realise they had.

Their answers are based on a broader consideration of life than simply the topic in hand. They are obliged to pull up from the detail and to draw upon their experiences in life so far. They look for general rules drawn from the wider world, and then apply them to a specific question. They are obliged to look within themselves for their personal wisdom.

In business consulting

A landscape gardening consultant recently visited my daughter Lucy and her husband to help plan a garden for their new home. Initially the consultant asked a series of practical questions about the garden, enquiring about the dimensions, soil type and gradient. Then she suddenly shifted gear. 'And what is the key image that you're looking for in your garden?' she asked. 'How would you describe the garden that you want to own?'

The whole tone of the conversation had dramatically changed. She was now asking them second questions. They were suddenly obliged to look deep within themselves to find the answers. They'd expected to be told how it was going be. Instead, they were being asked how they'd like it to be. An enforced period of surprisingly thoughtful and empowering reflection ensued.

Asking second questions of yourself

For you to become more aware of who you are and what you stand for, there needs to be an opportunity to reflect thoughtfully on yourself. The challenge is to pull together all of your subjective wisdom into a simple framework that highlights your key learnings and empowers you. Essentially, to know yourself better.

Self-reflection is a naturally occurring phenomenon. It occurs when we drive, when we lie in the bath or as we wait for a bus or an appointment. These enforced moments of 'time out' in our busy lives provide wonderful opportunities to briefly reflect upon ourselves. We can pull up from the business of responding to the immediate demands of the day and instead consider the bigger picture. 'What am I doing?' 'Where am I going?' And to clarify what's really important to us.

The problem with these fleeting opportunities is that they are usually interrupted by mundane events, and they rarely bring us to a satisfying conclusion or to a nuggety 'truth'. Unstructured self-reflection tends to be an exercise in worrying away at an issue, rather like a dog with a bone. Our minds go round and round without being led systematically to a concluding insight. We indulge in the activity of reflection without achieving a satisfying outcome. We tend to simply drift.

Often our personal reflections are based on a current worry (financial, health or work-related) and we simply ruminate endlessly about the facts. It is only when we discuss our worry with someone and have a structured conversation that we can move on. Hopefully our confidante will ask us good 'second questions' to help us start thinking.

For example, the accountant might ask us what our spending priorities are, the doctor might ask us what we need to change about our lives in order to improve our health and the boss might ask us what would make our work life more rewarding. These questions all lift up the conversation from the plain facts and prompt big picture reflection, helping you come up with an action plan based on an 'aha' moment.

The Power of the Second Question will help you to start thinking about your own second questions, and how you can find a greater depth and sense of fulfilment in life. Not only will this self-wisdom enrich your own life, but it will also help you elicit wisdom in those around you. You can learn how to invite children, partners, colleagues and friends to access their own wisdom, and to become more thoughtful and self-aware. In effect, you will learn how to lift up the level of conceptual awareness in others by inviting them to share a broader perspective with you.

Asking second questions of others is the absolute foundation of good teaching, good mentoring and good parenting. It is a hugely affirming skill that correlates highly with maturity and wisdom.

Dr Foster asked me a powerful second question during his visit to me. He obliged me to stop and to think conceptually about what I had learned in my professional life so far. He forced me to pause and to reflect on my key learnings. And when we are invited to lift up our thinking in this way, we are essentially being shown a fascinating pathway towards increased self-awareness.

It's a challenging path, but one that is well worth exploring.

Chapter One

REFLECTION, WISDOM AND INSIGHT

Reflection

The word 'reflection' means *to look back*, as if we are looking into a mirror or seeing our reflection in a pool of water. We are looking at ourselves as if from the outside. We are observing ourselves with a degree of detached curiosity. We are conducting a brief, objective review of our lives.

And sometimes when we look in the mirror, instead of just guiding the razor or applying some make-up, we might catch ourselves in the moment. We stop, we stare and we wonder just who is that person gazing so intently back at us?

In our quieter moments we all tend to become more reflective, thinking back over the day and pondering recent events. Usually we are looking back and reviewing facts, remembering what has happened and sorting the events into a coherent story.

Reflection usually occurs during the pauses in our lives, especially after an event has finished. Driving home from work, finishing reading a book or having a quiet glass of wine at the end of the day are all situations where we might drift into idle thought.

When we give ourselves a moment to stop *doing*, we can shift into a more detached state of *being*. We can be reflective, and we can passively dissect the day. The more 'in the moment' we are, the more reflective we become. Whether watching a sunset or gazing into an open fire, we all tend to become more aware of the bigger picture in our lives. We look for meaning, patterns or a sense of higher purpose.

We can all find ways to deliberately schedule more opportunities for reflection in our daily lives. We can keep a journal or diary, and choose a bath rather than a shower. Taking a regular walk at the end of the day is another simple way to unwind and reflect on the bigger picture. The habit of purposeful self-reflection is a skill that sets wise folk apart from the rest.

Holidays, funerals and school reunions — times for reflection

There are many opportunities for us to take the time out for more serious reflection. These are the times when we take the opportunity to stop, sit back and consider the bigger picture. They are times when we are struck by the broader sweep of our lives, and when we can access a deeper sense of personal awareness.

On holiday, it often takes a few days for the practical, everyday concerns to slip away and lose their significance. We stop texting or checking emails. We stop worrying about lists of things that we have to do. Instead, we start to ponder on the nature of life, on distant memories or on future dreams.

Our minds have become untethered and we tend to speculate more broadly on expansive issues.

At funerals, we sit and we remember. In our grief we are lifted up from everyday preoccupations and our thoughts range freely across broader landscapes. We enter a spiritual realm. We hear wonderfully succinct insights from speakers about aspects of the deceased and about the meaning of life. More importantly, for everyone at the service, this is also an opportunity to reflect at a personal level. It is another opportunity for big-picture thinking.

Finally, at school reunions, we usually find ourselves cringing at the effects of advancing age on our peer group. We trade competitive anecdotes and facts, and we see who's done well in life and who's fallen by the wayside. But behind the tittle-tattle of awkward interchanges, there lies opportunity. Firstly, it's a great opportunity to ask second questions of each other. But more importantly, on the way home, it's an even greater opportunity to reflect personally on the grander sweep of our lives — and to ask second questions of ourselves.

Reflection is a way of accessing a sense of wisdom in life. If we don't stop to reflect, then we simply trundle through the events that we experience without pause for thought, without assimilating what we have learned. We are little better than sheep, grazing with their noses firmly pressed to the ground for the entire duration of their life. And when they look up from the grass, they are simply looking for more grass.

There are naturally occurring moments of enforced big-picture reflection in life, usually *following adversity* when life comes to a crashing halt. Painful loss inevitably brings the burden of grief and a renewed search for purpose and meaning in life. In the eerie calm following a tragedy, we often experience profound insights about what is really important to us and what we truly value.

These life-changing insights also occur during those *exhilarating moments of joy*, when time seems to stand still. At the birth of a child or when we see the tail fluke of a diving whale against a picture-perfect sunset, we simply gaze in awe at the richness of life. We feel that we are in touch momentarily with something profound. We sense that there must be some kind of inherent message in the experience that connects us to a fundamental truth in life. We must grasp these opportunities with both hands whenever they occur.

Wisdom — more than just knowledge

We live in a world that sets a premium on information. It's a world of facts and figures. We learn facts from our parents, from TV and from our schooling through to university. The more that you know, the cleverer you seem.

It's a world that rarely seeks the *integrative overview*. These days society seems hell-bent on dumbing us down to a world of superficial facts. It is the exception rather than the rule when we are presented with a conceptual analysis of a problem. We live in a world where the media prefer to simply detail factual events, rather than to provide a contextual overview. We are served a diet of facts rather than concepts; information rather than ideas.

However, just knowing facts is only a part of the story. As we develop in our various roles we accumulate additional wisdom through our experience of life. This wisdom through experience cannot be taught; it cannot be formally learned.

Einstein once suggested that 'Learning is experience. Everything else is just information'. In this way, wisdom can be seen as the true knowledge that is gained through experience.

He also said, 'When I examine myself and my methods of thought, I come to the conclusion that the gift of fantasy has meant more to me than any talent for abstract, positive thinking. It was the ability to ask "What if?"'

In this way Einstein shows us that imagination and speculation beat factual knowledge every time in the quest for genuine wisdom.

Wisdom is usually associated with increasing age, but we all carry a unique personal wisdom regardless of our practical knowledge or life stage. Maturity does not necessarily equate with years of experience, but more often with time spent in thoughtful reflection. We often speak of young people carrying a wisdom beyond their years.

In many ways, the essence of this book is for each reader to access their own wisdom, and to achieve greater clarity about how the world operates through their own experience. However brief, however limited, and however tedious our lives might seem to us, we will all have had the opportunity to learn some profound lessons along the way.

We have not just experienced life – we have understood life.

Conventional champions of wisdom include philosophers such as Plato, Socrates, Sophia and Confucius. Socrates is famously quoted by Plato as saying that 'the unexamined life is not worth living', while another popular quote from ancient Greece (often attributed to Socrates) is the exhortation to 'know thyself'. Both of these comments emphasise the central role that self-awareness has to play in developing your personal wisdom.

Philosophers tend to distil their wisdom from one of two approaches; the *contemplative* and the *prudential* traditions.

Contemplative traditions, as used frequently by monks and nuns on retreat, emphasise reflection and meditation as the pathway to enlightenment. Conversely, *prudential traditions* emphasise the philosophical processes of logic that help us arrive at a considered opinion. We are asked to 'think' our way to a simple truth through deductive reasoning.

The book that you are now holding sits firmly in the *contemplative* corner of philosophical tradition. Discovering our personal wisdom does not require us to train in logical analysis or metaphysical reasoning. We are simply required to reflect quietly and to allow the insights to fall out of the silence that we have created for ourselves. A series of gentle second questions, asked quietly of ourselves, should be all that we need to find wisdom.

Finally, it should also be noted that there is much to be learned from *spiritual* guides, and from classic texts such as the Bible, the Qur'an, or scripts drawn from Taoist or Buddhist traditions. Spiritual enlightenment continues to be the most common pathway that people use when formally seeking big picture wisdom. Here, many second questions are asked in the search for purpose and meaning in our lives.

The wisdom that we seek in this way extends far beyond simple knowledge. It represents a profound sense of personal fulfilment. We don't just know things about life – we understand things about life.

Insight

Insight can be defined as a sudden understanding or a new perception of a complex situation. It involves a paradigm shift from *old think* to *new think*. We have all experienced moments of insight when, as a child, we 'understood' how to ride a bike or how to stand up or how to say 'Mama'. These 'aha' moments usually serve as markers of significant developmental milestones in our lives. Something has changed and we are the wiser for it.

Wisdom often comes to us in specific moments of insight when we suddenly realise a new simple truth that helps us make sense of the world. We gain a deeper understanding of life as a result. A 'light bulb' comes on and we are bathed in the illuminating moment.

There are many classic references to important, insightful moments in history. For example:

- When the Flat Earth Society realised that the world was round.
- When St Paul was blinded on the road to Damascus.
- When Archimedes shouted 'Eureka' in the bath.

These are all well-documented occasions when light-bulb moments occured. When 'the penny dropped' and when fundamental shifts in thinking occurred. These are the times when certain individuals realised something profound about the world and 'new truths' were established for the benefit of us all.

When we watch a detective thriller on TV, we often find that, towards the end, we suddenly realise that it wasn't the butler, but it was the gardener who killed the maid. All our previous assumptions about who was telling the truth are suddenly thrown into doubt. Along with the investigating officer, we surge along on an excitable wave of energy born of the 'aha'. With our new assumptions and core beliefs we see the world more clearly and it all makes greater sense.

Similarly, when we have a problem to solve, we struggle with the issue before a sudden realisation comes to us. We can see a way forward. We have an 'aha'. Whether we are trying to work out why the car won't start or how the DVD player operates, we all experience a mini 'aha' moment as we find the solution. Even remembering where you left your mobile phone usually involves a triumphant 'aha'.

These moments of sudden insight are often exquisite. They are the glitter and sparkle that light up our lives and drive the central theme of this book.

'Aha' moments are often delightful, almost magical experiences. They are always the product of a healthy curiosity, when an individual bothers to ask themselves clever questions in a search for a fresh perspective on their world. These expansive questions open new doors for us and as these doors reveal new vistas and insights, we can only gasp a knowing 'aha' in response.

Think of the excitable energy that accompanies parlour games such as charades or twenty questions. A small gathering of close family or friends will delight in collectively working its way towards a dawning realisation. Their progress is rarely linear. More often than not, after many false starts, a good question will suddenly elicit a collective 'aha' and everyone races joyously to the unveiling of the answer.

Finding insight is always satisfying. It is associated with a proud sense of achievement and of learning something new. It is not possible to have that flash of excitement without feeling energised and affirmed. This feeling can make 'aha' experiences extremely addictive. We are drawn to the intoxicating 'high' of the final reveal.

Remembering a personal 'aha' moment

Think back to a time when you experienced a major realisation in your life. A time when you had a transformational shift from feeling stuck to experiencing a surge of energy that propelled you forward. Perhaps it was a time when you decided to resign from a job or when you suddenly realised that you were free to make your own decisions. Describe it briefly below:

_____

_____

_____

_____

_____

Sit back and remember that feeling of lightness associated with the change. Was it a sense of relief tinged with excitement? The feeling that somehow you had opened a new door and that you now had a deeper understanding of who you were and what life was all about.

In his recent e-book, *The Brain and Emotional Intelligence: New Insights*, Daniel Goleman gives a fascinating account of the neurophysiology of an 'aha' moment. If you measure brainwaves during a creative moment, it turns out that there is intense gamma activity before the answer comes to us. Gamma activity indicates the binding together of neurons as a new association emerges. Immediately after that gamma spike, the new idea enters our consciousness.

This heightened activity during an insight focuses on the right temporal region. This is the same area of the brain that interprets metaphor and 'gets' jokes. It understands 'the language of poems, of art, and of myth'. It's the platform for dreams, where anything goes and the impossible seems possible.

The best way to mobilise this activity is to first concentrate intently on a problem and then relax. If you try to force an insight, as we all know, you will usually stifle the opportunity for a creative breakthrough.

Letting go is characterised by a high alpha rhythm, which signals mental relaxation, a state of openness, of daydreaming and drifting, where we're more receptive to new ideas. This sets the stage for the novel connections that occur during the gamma spike.

And when that moment of creativity occurs, we invariably experience a physical sensation of pleasure. We have our moment of joy and an ecstatic release. Gamma spikes are fun! They cost nothing and they bring a welcome vitality into our lives.

The spark that drives creativity

Elaine was the intelligent, personable director of a large academic program. During a particularly thought-provoking coaching session, we discussed a number of potential coaching goals to build greater creativity into her leadership role.

After some thoughtful discussion Elaine decided that she needed to:

- make more space for creativity in her work
- value and notice the power of creativity
- seek out more creative opportunities in her daily routines.

With a deep sigh, Elaine told me that creativity was the key factor that inspired her in life. She needed to nurture and enhance its role in the otherwise tedious list of roles and responsibilities that she held.

And just when I thought that we had reached a satisfying conclusion to our discussion, Elaine went on to add one further realisation:

'It seems to me that the spark behind all creativity is that magical moment of insight. That moment when you suddenly leap to an exciting new perspective on the familiar. I just love that feeling!'

Elaine was identifying a driving force behind her love of her work, and of life itself. She carried an unrelenting curiosity and search for new meaning that brought energy and vitality to her life. It was a perfect summary of the added joy that 'aha' moments can bring to our lives.

'Aha' moments are the key to the evolution of our civilisation. Just when we think that the world has plateaued and that things are settled, along comes another 'aha' or bright spark to help us jump forward. The invention of the wheel, of the internet, and the splitting of the atom inevitably involved a personal 'aha' moment for someone that propelled us all collectively forward towards the next evolutionary phase.

Inventions occur when someone is not satisfied with how things are and asks how things could be better. This is how technological evolution occurs and how social change comes about. One person asks a good question, experiences an 'aha', and then shares it with the world.

My five greatest insights

Insights are snappy, succinct one-liners that make immediate sense to you. They remind you of a personal truth in a concise and powerful way. They are inherently *wise*.

Write down as many simple one-line insights that you can remember having about life. For example, you may have suddenly realised that 'the more that I give, the more I receive'. Or that 'courage and fear go hand in hand'.

These one-liners might not come to you immediately, but you can always come back to your list and jot down ideas as you move through this book. Record your five favourite one-liners below:

1. _____

2. _____

3. _____

4. _____

5. _____

Insights are true nuggets of wisdom. They resonate strongly with your core values and beliefs, and provide wonderful foundation stones for constructing a coherent world view.

Summary

The modern world keeps us hooked on a diet of factual information, providing few invitations for us to reflect upon the bigger picture. Life is fast and we are not encouraged to stop and reflect on our experiences. We are all too busy doing practical things to contemplate more expansive ideas.

Increasingly, our social communication is pitched at the level of facts rather than ideas. We ask each other about the kids, about work and about recent events, but we rarely lift up conversations to consider more abstract ideas and concepts. And worse, we rarely bother to pause and ask ourselves what we've learned about life so far, or to notice how 'wise' we have become in our relatively brief time on the planet.

Everyone can reflect. Everyone can be wise. And everyone can have insights. It's actually a very simple formula to experience all this, but it requires us to use personal initiative to do so. If we make the time to reflect and ask challenging questions of ourselves, then more than likely we shall find satisfying answers. Increased personal wisdom becomes our reward.

Chapter Two

TECHNIQUES FOR TRADING WISDOM

When we think back to Dr Foster's Good Question (*What have you learned about people?*) we have the starting point for a wide range of useful questions to ask. We are moving from asking specific factual questions about details, to asking for an 'executive summary' or an overview. We are changing gear.

Second questions are designed to elicit abstract ideas. They are conceptual by nature and they seem expansive. But rather than inviting the respondent to talk at length on a wide range of topics, they instead require them to come up with a simple, almost factual summary statement. And for this reason they tend to distil their answers down to essential take-home 'truths'.

Socratic questioning

Socrates was a very wise man; perhaps one of the wisest men who ever lived. But his greatest contribution to philosophy was not his knowledge as such; rather it was his ability to ask good questions of others.

People would travel great distances to sit at his feet. They would come with questions or issues that they needed to be addressed. But they would not receive advice or answers to their questions. Instead, Socrates would reply by asking a good question of his own. He would ask a question that elicited an insight from the questioner. Essentially, he was inviting the person to find the answer to their own question.

By asking a thought-provoking question, Socrates was effectively holding up a mirror. By asking a logical series of questions, he would lead people to find their own 'aha' moment or insight about the way forward. They would be discovering wisdom within themselves of which they had been previously unaware. This was Socrates' greatest gift.

These days, Socratic questioning is a very popular mentoring style, found widely across all sectors of society. Often it happens naturally, for example, when interacting with children. Sometimes it needs to be a little more deliberate and structured, such as when teaching teenagers to consider the risks of certain socially exciting opportunities. It is far better to ask what the risks are if they stay out late, rather than to simply list the dangers for them.

During a formal de-briefing after a sporting event, a coach might ask players, 'And what have you learned from the game this afternoon?' Emergency services will also de-brief in a similar way after a callout. The team leader will elicit a critical review by asking the team what they thought they did well, what could have gone better and what else they might try next time. The team will be doing all the thinking. The leader is simply eliciting the ideas from them by asking good questions.

This process of inducing wisdom in others through asking good questions has now become the cornerstone of many professional interactions.

Socratic questioning is obviously a very common method in teaching. Instead of *telling* schoolchildren about some aspect of life, a teacher will *ask* them. If they struggle to find a reply, then a series of supplementary questions will gradually guide them to find the answer.

In this way schoolchildren are led to find their own answers, which they subsequently embrace as their own. They also learn to think critically along the way.

Teachers are encouraged to ask questions in a progressive series that lift up students' replies from the level of simple knowledge, to explore comprehension as a higher form of learning outcome. Each of these levels of questioning will induce a greater sense of wisdom in the student, as they search to find the answers within themselves rather than simply reiterating learned facts.

Clinical psychologists will also use Socratic questioning to systematically uncover a client's distressing pattern of thought. They will ask a series of 'why' questions until a key 'underlying assumption' is reached that underpins the negative thinking. The idea is that a whole range of negative thoughts emanates from a core dysfunctional belief that feels true to the client, but is not helpful to them. By holding up a mirror to invite reflection, the psychologist induces a transformational 'aha' moment for the client and new insight is gained.

All therapy techniques can be seen as attempts to induce a new 'wisdom' for the client. Invariably, by asking challenging questions, we will promote thoughtful reflection with a consequent realisation that things could be different.

An external business consultant will use a very similar questioning process to induce change. The consultant will usually know very little about the company's business, but will be skilled at asking the right questions. They will almost deliberately adopt the position of a naive enquirer.

The process is the same, but the language is intriguingly different. While psychologists like to conceptualise their questions as leading their client 'downwards' towards an underlying core insight, business consultants prefer the notion of 'lifting up' the analysis to a conceptual overview. They talk of 'helicopter views' and 'blue skies' visioning. They like to see over the horizon and, in general, use far more expansive metaphors in their work. They talk about stepping back and working 'on' the business rather than 'in' the business.

They will ask questions such as:

- If we could look down on your business from on high, what would we see?
- If we could fast forward to five years from now, where would we be?
- If we could dream of a perfect world, what would your business look like?

The core technique is to *ask good questions* that provoke insight and wisdom, rather than to *give good advice*. This is the essence of the Socratic method.

Delivering wisdom to the farm gate

Murray was a salesman/farm advisor who travelled around rural areas reviewing farming practices with local farmers. As they leaned on the gate they would talk about all manner of things, but mostly facts. They would discuss stock prices, legislative change and the weather. Essentially, Murray was there to make a sale, but he was bored.

Somehow Murray needed to lift up the level of conversation for his work to become more stimulating and less repetitive. He wanted to know what really motivated and inspired his clients. We decided that all he really needed to do was to ask!

- What makes farming such a fulfilling role for you?
- Why are you so passionate about farming?
- What's the most inspiring thing that's happened since we last met?
- What do you think is the key attribute of a good farmer?

The list of Murray's second questions went on and on. Lifting up from the facts and wheeling around some big-picture topics gave significantly more grunt to the conversations. The sense of connection was stronger, and the genuine interest in his customers' replies gave a greater authenticity to Murray's visits. Suddenly both parties were looking forward to the next visit. Murray was no longer just selling farm products, he was trading ideas.

Kolb's Learning Cycle

In recent years it has become very popular to conceptualise a series of reflective questions as a cycle. These are sometimes called *learning conversations* and are based on a simple model initially proposed by David Kolb in 1984. The cycle describes the basic technique for trading wisdom and extracting wise 'ahas' from others. When applied as a process of self-reflection, it becomes a powerful technique for discovering personal insights.

Kolb proposed that experiential learning can be conceptualised in a four-stage *learning cycle* as outlined below. Initially drawn from an educational setting, it has been widely applied to a huge range of clinical and business development processes.

The learning process involves moving around the circle asking a series of deliberate questions, usually starting at the *concrete experience* stage. This involves the teacher/mentor/therapist or supervisor asking for a factual account of what happened. It might concern a specific problem or a troubling theme in life.

KOLB'S LEARNING CYCLE

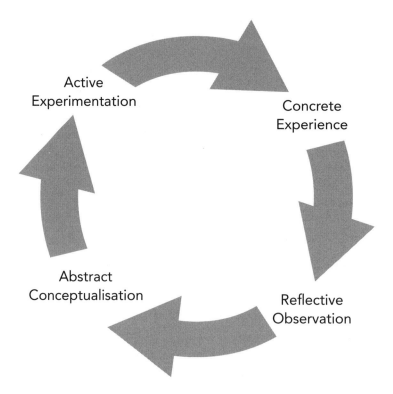

Once this has been clearly and objectively described, we move on to the *reflective observation* stage. Here, we reflect on the context of the event and the meaning or function that it might have in our lives.

We then move on to the *abstract conceptualisation* stage, where we extract the simple truths or nuggety learnings that help us carry forward a generically useful insight. This is the stage where the powerful second questions are asked and genuine wisdom is induced.

Finally we move to the *active experimentation* stage where the new conceptualisation is tested out in the real world. This usually takes the form of a 'homework' exercise.

At each stage of this logical process, structured questions are used to carry the student/client/supervisee around the circle. Once completed, the cycle starts again.

Examples of good questions at each stage of the cycle include:

- Concrete experience: What happened? Who was involved?
- Reflective observation: What is the pattern? What were the triggers?
- Abstract conceptualisation: What can you learn from all this? What does it mean for you?
- Active experimentation: How can you test out your new idea?

It is critically important to note that this cycle is driven by a series of questions, and by the questions alone. Under no circumstances should the mentor break rank and 'give advice' to the supervisee. Although at times it might seem frustrating in the extreme to let people come slowly to their own answers when the answer seems obvious to the questioner, we must never become *prescriptive*. Although it often seems quicker to just tell others what to do and jump to suggesting an answer, it steals the moment for self-discovery.

Kolb's Learning Cycle provides a great structure to drive the Socratic method described earlier. We move from asking factual questions (*What happened?*) to a series of second questions (*How does this fit into your life? What does it mean?*), and then finally we ask a very practical type of question again (*What will you do?*).

When we are trying to put structure into our own self-reflection, we should use this process to help us come to an insightful conclusion. All too often when we indulge in reflection, we simply ruminate endlessly about the factual event. We drift off into unstructured and vacuous 'if onlys' or 'what ifs', but never seem to extract the core insights. Nor do we evolve a practical plan for moving forward.

You can use the panel below to address a simple problem in your own life by using the learning cycle:

_____

Using Kolb's Learning Cycle to guide your self-reflection

Think about a simple problematic event that has occurred recently in your life. Or it could be a recurrent issue that is troubling you.

- What is the problem? _____

  _____

- What is the wider issue? _____

  _____

- What is the key learning in this for you? _____

  _____

- What can you do differently next time? _____

  _____

Notice how the series of structured questions leads you to both a personal insight (a key learning) and a practical plan for change.

_____

Reasoning — deductive and inductive

There are two types of reasoning processes, and they both require us to ask a progressive series of questions.

Deductive reasoning obliges us to work logically through a series of steps towards an inevitable end point, seeking to arrive at hard facts or knowledge. Wisdom, especially *prudential wisdom* (see Chapter One) can be found using deductive reasoning. We can use deductive reasoning to analyse the events in our lives and to extract a broadly applicable conclusion. An example might be: 'Every time I sit near a cat I get itchy. Therefore I must be allergic to cats.'

In contrast, *inductive reasoning* requires us to make a series of intuitive leaps, asking speculative second questions that take us towards a world of possibility. It can lead us to the most brilliant of insights and ideas, but it can also trip us up. We are using hypothesis and speculation to discover new possibilities, but our insights are far more likely to be flawed. For example, we might think, 'If I get in to work earlier, then I will be able to leave earlier.' We reason that the earlier we start, the earlier we will finish. This may or may not be true!

Second questions can be used as part of both deductive and inductive processes. They can pull in new information from left field to assist in a deductive train of thought, but more often they will be seen as an integral part of an intuitive leap forwards. Weather forecasts are classic examples of inductive reasoning, where the forecasters review all of the available facts and make bold predictions based on them. They will have asked themselves a series of thought-provoking questions based on the patterns and trends that they see. They seem authoritative and wise, but sometimes it can appear to be just guesswork.

In fact, *guessing* is simply an extreme example of desperately speculative inductive reasoning, where we attempt to predict outcomes based on little or no valid information.

Faulty inductive reasoning is rife in both casinos and at the races. It is also rife among speculators on the share market, which just shows how strongly we can hold to the apparent validity of a firm belief in defiance of logic. There is a fine line between a wise person and a fool!

When inductive reasoning goes well, however, wonderful things happen. Detectives make spectacular leaps to solve crimes and traders on Wall Street correctly anticipate share price fluctuations. They cannot *know* what will happen, but they do know what *has* happened and they can make connections based on their experience. They seem *wise* and we admire them for it.

Inductive reasoning requires us to create a general truth to help guide our logic. It has to be a *best fit* assumption, and we will never know for sure that it is true. However, it opens the door to potential solutions, and it frees us up from the facts.

To do this, we need to become more aware of the general rules and themes on which we base our leaps of faith. It's not just a 'gut feeling' or intuition that drives us. There are underlying assumptions that drive our decisions. To manage ourselves well in uncertain situations we need to know what we believe in. At times like these, facts are not enough.

Intuitive thinking

Intuitive thinking is best described as part of the Myers–Briggs Type Indicator (MBTI), one of the most popular personality assessment tools that is currently available. Initially designed by Isabel Briggs Myers and her mother Katharine Briggs, it is based on a Jungian model of personality type. It has spawned many variants, but essentially it identifies four dichotomies that define personality type: Introversion/Extraversion, Intuitive/Sensing, Thinking/Feeling, and Perceiving/Judging.

It is not the purpose of this book to launch into a major review of the Myers–Briggs theory, but it is of great interest here for us to consider just one of the four dichotomies: the *intuitive world view* versus the *sensing world view*.

This dichotomy highlights the role of big-picture thinking in life, in contrast to a focus on practical details.

Sensing types see the world as it is. They prefer to deal in facts and they use their five senses to sift information. They focus on background knowledge and tradition. They are very practical people.

Conversely, *intuitive* types see future possibilities and ideas. They prefer to look ahead and see connections between things. They use a sixth sense to access what is not actually present and will follow a *hunch* in search of a solution. They inhabit the big-picture world of ideas and concepts.

Intuitive types with a passion for 'things' will be drawn to conceptual ideas which use logic to think outside the square. Intuitive types who love 'feelings' will be drawn to inspiration and expansive visions. The common theme is that all intuitive types look beyond the present facts and practical challenges, and see something compelling ahead of them.

Sensing types can see intuitive types as wistful dreamers, while intuitive types see sensing types as pedantic and dull. In reality, we all need a balance of both, regardless of a personal tendency towards one style or the other. The goal of this book is very much to encourage *intuitive thinking,* in that insight and 'aha' moments only really occur when we are in this space.

The MBTI offers a number of practical techniques for encouraging intuition:

- Start looking for 'patterns' and connections between events.
- Encourage 'flights of ideas'.
- Ask yourself what something reminds you of.
- Ask more questions beginning with 'if'.
- Play word association games.
- Encourage fantasy and daydreams.
- Use metaphor.
- Explore your creativity.

- Speculate more about future possibilities.
- Make decisions based on 'gut feelings' rather than logic.
- Encourage your imagination.
- Develop an interest in abstract art and poetry.

All of the above suggestions can easily be translated into second questions such as:

- What is your gut feeling about this?
- If the barriers to change came down, how do you imagine your world would look?
- What is the pattern here?
- What does this remind you of?

Intuitive thinkers love problem solving. They love to gnaw away at conceptual issues. They like change, surprise and innovation. They love the 'aha' moments that come from making intuitive leaps.

Abstract versus concrete thinking

All thinking can be divided into two types: abstract and concrete. *Concrete thinkers* live in the objective world of practical facts and tangible things. *Abstract thinkers* use concepts rather than facts and generalise away from the information in front of them to consider broader principles and ideas.

Most planning or design work involves abstract thought. We ask 'what might be?' But then the implementation or actual creation requires concrete thinking skills. This is the essential difference between *builders* and *architects* in their complementary approaches to building a house.

When we reflect upon our lives and who we are, it is useful to adopt the perspective of a big-picture planner or designer and ask the kind of questions that they might ask. 'Who am I?' does not require the answer of 'A 40-year-old Caucasian mother of two'. Instead, the question needs to lift us up from simple facts to find a more abstract and telling definition.

'I am a determined campaigner for social justice' or 'I am the heart of my family' are examples of simple personal statements that people have shared with me recently. Both descriptions involve abstraction from facts and both give strong messages about personal values.

Abstract concepts are the cornerstone of the creative arts. Abstract art typically requires the observer to 'see' things beyond the canvas. We are invited to abstract our own meaning from the work. We are looking outside the square and are thinking more expansively about what we see. It's a great place to find insight.

Similarly, we are often told that 'it's not what's on the lines, but between the lines' that is important in a written message. Don't take the message at face value. Often it's not what is said but what is not said that is the crucial information.

For example, the most evocative aspects of great movies are the scenes that fade to grey, leaving us to use our imagination to come up with an ending based on what has gone before. Conversely, movies that leave nothing to the imagination are not quite the exquisite experience that we might hope for. The real joy of watching a movie is to let our minds drift; to abstract ourselves from the immediate story and let the ideas and themes resonate with aspects of our own lives.

Builders who can dream

There is a well-known story about three men all building with bricks. The first man was asked what he was doing and he grumpily said that he was carrying bricks. The second man said, in a tired sort of way, that he was building a wall. Finally, the third man replied enthusiastically that he was building a fantastic cathedral; the most beautiful that the world had ever seen.

> Sometimes we need to lift up our heads a little from the here and now in order to find true fulfilment in life. Sometimes it helps for us to see the bigger picture.

Summary

We have looked at several key techniques for trading wisdom. By holding up the mirror we can use general Socratic questioning techniques to prompt self-reflection and to elicit inspirational 'aha' moments.

Kolb's Learning Cycle builds on this and gives us a very practical framework for structuring the process. We move from initial fact finding to subsequent big-picture questions that ask about context and meaning. By capturing the inherent lessons in our answers we can dramatically increase our self-awareness and our worldly wisdom.

We have seen how second questions tend to be asked as part of an inductive reasoning process. They invite us to think in abstract concepts rather than concrete facts and are preferred by those who think intuitively.

We can all learn how to embrace these techniques and to celebrate the power of big-picture conceptual thinking. We can learn to pull together our key learnings from the past in this way and we can also allow ourselves to visualise the future with confidence. As a result of this we will seem more than simply knowledgeable; we will also seem wise.

Chapter Three

GOOD QUESTIONS TO ASK

In the previous chapter we considered a number of techniques for eliciting 'aha' moments by asking good questions, both of ourselves and of others. We now need to find a simple way of organising and cataloguing these questions into usable forms. Just what do these questions look like and how do they sound?

In this chapter we will consider a range of good questions to ask, arranged according to their structure. But before we do, consider the following exercise. It invites you to take some time to look and listen to the world around you, and to notice the second questions that you hear.

A brief survey of second questions in your own world
Set aside 10 to 15 minutes of your time to listen for second questions

in your own world. Take a notepad and record any examples of second questions from radio, TV or in conversations between friends, family or colleagues. If you wish, sit in a café and listen out for them.

Listen for moments when the respondent has to pause, reflect and summarise their reply with a nuggety truth.

Situation	The second question	The wise reply
_____	_____	_____
_____	_____	_____
_____	_____	_____
_____	_____	_____
_____	_____	_____

In reviewing the frequency of second questions in your social world, you may be surprised at your findings. You may find that you are swimming in a rich sea of clever questions. Conversely, you may find that everyone is plodding along in a conceptual desert, devoid of insights and higher order thinking. Either way, you will have become more aware of your social environment and the opportunities that arise to think more expansively and open up conversations to a different level.

Dr Foster goes to (the super) market

Henry had been working as a checkout operator in a local supermarket after school. Being a teenage boy he was generally reluctant to share any news about his day.

As we drove to school one morning I decided to ask him Dr Foster's Good Question verbatim. It seemed certain to open up an interesting dialogue.

'Henry, in the six months that you have been working at the supermarket checkout, what have you learned about people?'

There was an agonising silence before his cutting reply, 'Well, Dad. There are two kinds of people in this world. There are those who like small talk and there are those that don't. And I don't!'

And that was that! He had given me a succinct, nuggety reply that fulfilled all of the technical aspects of a wise reply, but that also sat uncomfortably as a classic teenage rebuttal of a polite adult enquiry. It was also Henry's truth. We drove on in a thoughtful silence, both quietly reflecting on his wryly provocative insight.

The style for asking good questions of others

In asking a second question, we often pause thoughtfully and become more deliberate in our style. We are mining for a deeper truth and by slowing down the information flow we can invite a thoughtful reply. We are implying, 'Now think carefully before you answer this'. We are moving to a more philosophical level of communication.

Any question, if phrased carefully, can develop a special power and elicit the extra magic that defines them as a second question. Second questions occur at the point in a conversation where we stop looking for factual answers and instead pull back to set up a question that requires a more abstract response. We ask a question where the answer will require the respondent to pause and think before delivering a more thoughtful reply.

When we ask second questions of others, we should always maintain a sense of genuine interest in the possibility of eliciting a wise reply. We should adopt a position of non-judgmental curiosity about the other person, genuinely seeking to find out more about them. As the line of enquiry unfolds, in particular, when the second question hits, the 'aha' moment almost becomes a shared gift. Both the questioner and the respondent can feel a sense of delight in the mutual discovery of the simple truth.

You can practise your style of questioning at any time by asking a friend or family member a couple of simple questions about their day.

Asking simple second questions

When you next meet a friend, colleague or family member, ask them three simple questions:

1. What have you been up to today?
2. What's been the best bit?
3. And why did you enjoy it so much?

Inevitably the 'why' question (a second question) will invite them to extract a simple wisdom about themselves. It will not require debate or evaluation, it will simply be a short statement of 'fact' that you can both subsequently reflect further upon at your leisure.

The structure of second questions

Good prefaces to use

Questions are usually defined by the nature of their first word. *Who, what, why, where* and *how* are all common kinds of questions that we might ask. Most of them simply drive the respondent towards disclosing factual information, much as we might expect a detective to ask of a suspect or a parent to ask of a child. In the quest for wisdom these are essentially looseners or first questions.

But second questions are different. Usually it is the introductory phrase that makes the question so much more expansive, setting the scene for a more insightful reply. Consider the following prefaces to a range of 'what' questions:

- *At the end of the day*, what have you learned?
- *Of everything that we've discussed*, what's the key issue for you?
- *Taking everything into account*, what is the most significant aspect for you?
- *If you look back over everything that's happened*, what jumps out as your major learning outcome?
- *If there was one thing that you could tell your children*, what would it be?
- *If you had one wish*, what would it be?
- *If your mother were here*, what would she advise?
- *When you pull everything together*, what is the simple take-home message for you?

In each case, the preface lifts up our expectations for a more expansive reply. We are homing in on wisdom.

Good prefaces to a question

Brainstorm a personal list of prefaces to questions that you could use in conversation with others. The more that you work on developing this aspect of your interpersonal style, the more insightful discussions you will have.

1. Prefaces that reference *time*

When you look back ...

Of all the things that you've learned about ...

_____

_____

_____

2. Prefaces that reference current *context*

When you look around at everything that's going on …

Of all the things that you can see around you …

_____

_____

_____

3. Prefaces that explore *possibilities*

If you had a magic wand …

Supposing you were blindfolded …

_____

_____

_____

_____

_____

_____

Developing a range of good prefaces to use with your questions will automatically enrich the quality of your subsequent interactions with others.

Open-ended questions

It almost goes without saying that second questions should be open-ended in style. We are asking the other person to open up and trying to avoid eliciting simple yes/no answers. By definition, open-ended questions should allow space for the respondent to provide their own input into the debate.

An open-ended question is designed to encourage a full, meaningful answer using the subject's own knowledge and/or feelings. It is the opposite of a *closed question*, which encourages a short or single-word answer. Open-ended questions also tend to be more genuinely curious about the opinions of others and seem less leading and perfunctory than closed questions.

'Tell me about your day at school?' sets up a far broader and more wide-ranging disclosure than 'Did you go to school today?'

In asking open-ended questions, we will always leave a meaningful pause to allow the other person to reflect and gather their thoughts before replying. When we notice people pausing in this way it is invariably a sign that we are asking good questions.

Summary questions

Many second questions have a sense of conclusion or integration about them. We are inviting the other person to wrap up the conversation with an overview.

'Now that we've had this conversation …' or 'Having considered everything we've discussed so far …' would be typical examples of questions that invite a pulling together of the key points. By asking for the key points, we will usually extract a short list of nuggety abstractions that represent an over-arching summary of the facts.

Many supervision sessions, business consultations and counselling sessions will end with a very common question: 'What are the *key issues* that you can extract from our conversation today?'

Key issues are always succinct. We are distilling the simple take-home message from a conversation. If we fail to summarise and integrate our learnings in this way, the facts alone will simply fade with time. Ideally, we always pull such purposeful conversations together with a summary question that extracts the key insights, which are often being consciously considered for the first time.

A question has been asked

On internet auction websites such as eBay or TradeMe, any item put up for sale usually has a few questions asked about it by viewers online. They are always factual and usually dull, such as 'How heavy is it?' or 'When was it last serviced?'

But there is no reason why any reader of this book couldn't run riot around the same items for sale, asking more intriguing second questions of the seller. Such as:

- What is your favourite memory about owning the car?
- If you could say one thing about the fridge that you really liked, what would it be?
- What's the most poignant photo that you ever took on that camera?

Asking these kinds of second questions would have shifted the conversation up from the tittle-tattle of marketplace facts and into a wider world of trading exquisite, often highly insightful, experiences. We are opening a door into an altogether more colourful and thought-provoking world.

Questions that lift you up

As noted previously, business consultants like to *lift up* conversations to allow for an executive overview of the world. They talk of wide horizons, blue skies and helicopter views. Essentially they conceptualise big-picture thinking as a process of looking down from above and gaining insights that are simply not possible when we are immersed in the terrestrial world of facts and detail.

The view from the top somehow seems so much more insightful (especially when you happen to be at the top!). Gazing down at the world from the window of a plane is almost invariably a time of personal big-picture reflection.

The concept of *pulling up from the detail* to consider the bigger picture is widely used in everyday conversation. Often, when we are grappling with a problem, we will pull up from the detailed analysis and step back for a while, taking a fresh look from a distance. When we are arguing, we will pull up from the specific disagreement to remind ourselves of the broader points of agreement.

Looking down on oneself is an excellent perspective from which to gain personal insight and increased self-awareness. Inviting a conceptual overview is also a great style of question to use.

Questions that dig deep

Another popular conceptualisation for asking penetrating questions is to imagine that we are *digging deep* to uncover nuggets or gems that lie within us. We are mining for the 'aha' moments. Therapists often talk in this way.

In more general discussion we may often hear phrases such as 'What lies beneath all this?' or 'What's the key idea that underpins all this?' The idea that a bigger unifying concept lies *beneath* a range of factual details is a compelling way of making sense of information and finding meaning in it.

Often when we are looking inwards, or inside ourselves, the metaphor of *digging deep* is used. When someone introspects in a search for meaning we often say that they are going deep within themselves. In contrast to the expansive search for meaning in the heavens or blue skies, we are looking for wisdom in the depths of our soul. Here we find fundamental truths, cornerstone beliefs and anchoring concepts.

Our wisdom from digging deep seems rock-solid in a way that breezy aerial dreams will never manage to replicate.

We go deep to find authenticity. We fly high to find inspiration.

Questions that look back

Most wisdom and insight is drawn from past experience; it is the inherent nature of reflective thinking. We look back and consider all that we have learned in life so far. The phrase 'insight from hindsight' captures the situation perfectly. Second questions that look back are necessarily couched in the past tense, and they will usually begin with the word 'when'.

Good retrospective questions do not simply ask for facts, such as 'When did you leave school?' Instead they invite the respondent to reflect on a more abstract concept, usually involving an insight such as:

- When did you first realise that you were no longer a child?
- When did you know that you had truly reached adulthood?

Both of these questions require that the respondent conducts a brief review of their life so far and then extracts their own marker for the transition. They will usually come up with a pleasing personal anecdote that captures the essence of what adulthood means to them. There will be an inherent sense of wisdom about adulthood in the story.

I first realised that I was an adult when I came across a serious road accident. There was no-one to tell me what to do. I had to take personal responsibility for the lives of a couple who were trapped. I could see it in their eyes. They were looking to me as their saviour.

This (hypothetical) anecdote sets up a wonderfully profound observation that can subsequently be used as a wise comment by both the questioner and the respondent (and now even you the reader!). We can all say:

- Sometimes, we know when we are acting as responsible adults; we can see it in other people's eyes.

Or:

- We know that we've come of age when we realise that others depend on us to act responsibly.

These abstractions can be incredibly useful insights to share with others in future conversations. We are sharing wisdom.

Questions that look forward

In contrast to retrospective questions, forward-looking questions allow us to drift expansively across future possibilities. We are sailing into the vast unknown, boldly speculating about how the future might look. This is the theatre for developing a personal vision or to set strategic plans and objectives for ourselves.

- If you jumped forward to five years from now, what would you see?
- When you are facing your final few moments, what will your legacy be?
- How would you prefer things to be?

These are all simple yet challenging questions that are also often asked in therapy. Clients can become so preoccupied with the specific problems of the moment that they don't take the time to look ahead and see a way forward.

An overriding theme to a good therapeutic conversation is to move steadily from an initial retrospective review of past events towards a more forward-looking planning process. To gradually shift from asking about 'what happened' to asking about 'how things could be'.

Questions that ask what we don't even know we know (also known as blind-spot questions)

'If' questions can open the door to a vast array of wisdom that the bearer doesn't even know they carry! A classic question that a very challenging therapist friend of mine used to ask was: 'If you knew the answer to your problem, what would it be?' Sadly, the usual response was along the lines of: 'Well, I wouldn't be coming here to see you for a start!'

Astute readers will note that embedded within most 'if' questions is usually a 'what' question. 'If' takes us out into the speculative world and from there we can look for insight and wisdom with our usual array of challenging questions.

Sometimes during performance reviews or in coaching sessions we are asked to identify personal blind spots, shadow sides and vulnerabilities. These are always hard to see in ourselves as we tend to minimise or deny them, especially when they are pointed out by our nearest and dearest.

Although it is true that 'We know what we know and we usually know what we don't know', sometimes 'we don't know what we know' and, worse still, 'we don't know what we don't know!' It is here, floundering in the dark, where we usually find the most powerful of our light-bulb moments.

Accessing wisdom from the subconscious is tricky. If we are unaware, we are unlikely to ask ourselves the right questions that lead to an 'aha'. Often, we too quickly dismiss the opportunity with the classic line: 'I don't know.' However, with a little more application, it is amazing how much we can discover about ourselves and the world, and how much is not so much a matter of factual knowledge but more a matter of simply becoming aware.

As newborn infants, none of us knows what to do. We haven't been told.

We gradually work it all out for ourselves. We don't know about healthy diets or what lies outside of our cot. But we quickly acquire a world view and a skillset that is influenced massively by our limited experience to that point in time. We don't exactly ask ourselves questions at that stage of life, but we extrapolate from our experience, we generalise, and we draw inferences about things of which we are unaware.

Our trial-and-error approach to illuminating our world brings a daily cascade of insights as we discover new things. For the newborn, every day is a rich learning experience where delightful insights happen with almost every move.

The Johari Window

A common framework for asking blind-spot questions is called the Johari Window (Luft and Ingham, 1955). Here, it's represented as a simple matrix that offers us the structure to ask questions that may not occur to us alone. They relate to things that others might see about us or even things that neither others nor ourselves might know.

	Known to self	Not known to self
Known to others	Public arena	Personal blind spot
Not known to others	Private façade	Unknown (potential)

The Johari Window has become a standard way of cataloguing any number of issues concerning the public and private divide. It sets the scene for some very interesting and thought-provoking discussions between participants.

The most intriguing area for exploration is that described as 'unknown' to both self and others, sometimes referred to as the subconscious. Questions asked in this area are always speculative, difficult to test, and they are impossible to answer definitively. Psychoanalysts spend a great deal of time poking around in this quadrant, asking open-ended questions in the hope of flushing out an 'aha' moment for the client.

Eliciting an insight which was not previously known to either party is a richly satisfying experience.

> One does not become enlightened by imagining figures of light, but by making the darkness conscious. Carl Gustav Jung

Almost by definition, the most dramatic 'aha' moments will occur around questions directed at the void of the unknown. This is the area where a single light-bulb moment can dramatically illuminate our blind ignorance.

Speculative questions

'Why …' is a compelling question to ask, but it is also open to myriad speculative answers. 'Why' questions sound so focused, but invariably they simply invite the respondent to offer up any amount of uncertain answers. The most likely answer is always going to be 'I don't know'.

Why is the sky blue? would be the classic why question. If people knew why, they would be famous. It is a big-picture question that invites an expansive reply, but sadly the answer is always slightly lame.

Asking 'why' questions can be seen as a quest for meaning or purpose in life. We are looking to set an observation about the world into a wider context than our own knowledge base can logically explain.

'Why' questions are the foundation questions that underpin many spiritual and psychotherapeutic endeavours. 'Why am I insecure?' invites a range of theories about childhood, genetics and social influences. However, we are simply speculating about causes and we will never know for sure that we are right.

Science appears to try and address 'why' questions too, but usually by asking more pedantic 'what' or 'how' questions. We will never know for sure 'why' gravity pulls the Earth around the Sun, but we do know more and more about 'how' it does and 'what' happens as a result.

Following the devastating earthquake in Christchurch, New Zealand, a televised discussion was held about the possible designs for a new cathedral. The debate focused largely on whether it was safe to build a new spire, and if so, what materials should be used. Suddenly the level of debate was lifted significantly when one panel member observed: 'Surely, the question is not really *what type* of spire the cathedral needs. Instead, we should be asking ourselves *why* the cathedral needs a spire?'

This question dramatically changed the nature of the conversation, lifting the debate to a significantly higher level. Participants collectively 'changed gear'. They had moved from a pragmatic consideration of the re-build to a discussion of the role architecture plays in enhancing spiritual practice.

It was a grand example of a second question in action!

Most questions asked in the search for religious or spiritual meaning are speculative by nature. The answers that we are looking for are simply too huge for us to ever be able to validate. Instead, we look to generate a set of subjective facts that help us make sense of the human condition. To do this, we usually rely on a mixture of received wisdom and self-evident truths that we distil from our experiences so far.

In many ways, 'why' questions are the most compelling and ambitious of all second questions, but they are also the hardest to answer. Asking 'why' is probably the most frequently asked question of this type and it is usually the least satisfactorily answered.

Summary

In this chapter we have reviewed a variety of structures and technical aspects of second questions. Asking the questions with a healthy curiosity is important, and prefacing our words with a broad introduction is crucial. Making open-ended invitations to both reflect and to summarise is also important.

We can invite others to look back, to look forward, to fly high or to dig deep. We can come at the search for meaning in any number of ways, most typically by asking 'why'.

At the end of the day we can see that there are myriad good questions to ask. And now that we know what they are we have no excuse not to start using them, both in conversations with others and in personal reflection with ourselves.

Chapter Four

COLOURFUL TECHNIQUES FOR CAPTURING 'AHA' MOMENTS

'Aha' moments should be savoured. They are energising, satisfying and they lie at the cutting edge of personal development. They describe significant moments of insight when wisdom can flourish. Not surprisingly, delightful surprises are often elicited by colourful techniques.

Using metaphor

The most colourful way of lifting up your thoughts from the here and now is to make reference to similar situations that you are reminded of. The connection sparks other similarities and a new awareness falls into place. Many examples can be found in everyday speech. When we describe a child's room as a pig's sty, we are recognising all the qualities that are similar between the two situations and a number of additional insights will inevitably occur as a result.

This is an example of a metaphor, a figure of speech which is not literally applicable, but that suggests a resemblance. It is a description that is commonly used by us all. If a metaphor involves the word 'like', it is called a simile.

Many years ago a client who was going through a difficult legal separation involving many different professional opinions told me that he felt like he was 'flying a Lancaster bomber in World War II'. He was lumbering along in the dark, drawing flak from all sides. He told me that he was confused and scared, and his only available response was to drop his bombs randomly and angrily wherever he could. He was out of control, but could see no other options for his survival. With this simple metaphor he was able to convey a thousand different aspects of his situation and also find potential solutions to his problems.

Another client once described her traumatised life as being like 'a wonderful sandy beach that had been covered in rubbish and the wreckage from a violent storm'. But each day, as the tides came in and then went out, nature slowly brought order to the chaos. It was a great metaphor to work with, adding substance to the old maxim that 'time will surely heal'.

The interesting thing about metaphors is that we can 'trade' them. After seeing the client who was going through the traumatic separation, I was able to use his description with several other clients, in order to help validate their own situation and also to provide potential suggestions for change.

Passing on other people's metaphors is a tricky business. When it works, it's a powerful contribution to a conversation, providing many potential insights. However, with poor timing, or to someone who doesn't know what flying a Lancaster bomber would be like, the metaphor will go down like a lead balloon [sic!].

In finding wise metaphors of our own, we need to open our awareness to our past experiences and consider what a situation reminds us of. This comes more easily to some of us than others, but it is a simple habit that we can all learn.

If we look outside the square for a situation that resonates with the situation in hand, we will usually find something that we can use. A good metaphor, drawn from a parallel situation, can provide wonderful 'aha' moments. The automatic connection sparks insight.

Finding metaphors for life situations

Consider a situation where you have so much to do that you don't know where to start. Everywhere you look, all you can see are things that need to be done. What metaphor could you use to describe your situation? What does the situation remind you of?

Example: It's like:

_____

_____

_____

_____

Metaphor is a great source of insight. There are many metaphors that are commonly used to describe life and each has a value of its own. We often hear about the river of life or the suggestion that life is a journey, but a metaphor that I commonly use is to suggest that a person's life story is like a 30-chapter book. I suggest that they might currently be in chapter ten, and I remind them that they are the *lead characters in their own life story (something that we often forget!)*. Characters come and go from one chapter to the next and certain things happen as the story unfolds. Once the structure is in place I then ask them the following questions:

- What is the title of your book?
- What are the essential qualities of the main character?
- What is the basic theme that the reader can admire and learn from?

A similar metaphor might refer to life as a 'three-act play', with five scenes in each. Again, the plot unfolds, but understanding the central character is the key goal of the analysis.

My life as a book with 30 chapters

If my life were to be the subject of a 30-chapter novel, which chapter would I be in right now? Answer the following questions about the story:

1. The *title* of my book is:

_____

_____

2. The main *theme* of my book is:

_____

_____

3. The prime *qualities* of the lead character are:

_____

_____

_____

As you fill in the blank spaces above, remember that you can choose how you describe your life story and you can choose how you wish the synopsis to read.

By deliberately using metaphor more often and hitching supplementary questions to them, we can elicit surprising and often delightful moments of insight.

Using anecdote

An anecdote is a short description of a particular incident or occurrence that is personally interesting. When we share personal anecdotes, or describe real-life stories that we have heard or experienced in the past, we offer opportunities for others to gain insight. As someone tells you of their predicament, you might remember something similar that happened to you or to someone else that you know of. There is usually a key message or learning to extract.

As with metaphor, the use of anecdote can prove reassuring when delivered appropriately, but can also distract the conversation inappropriately away from the immediate concerns of the other person. They simply might not want to hear that you've had similar problems when they're trying to let off their own steam. Sometimes, however, sharing a similar experience allows for a hugely reassuring and comforting moment in others. They know that you know what they are feeling. You have been there too. And they can see their own situation more clearly through the parallels that can be drawn. They often gain personal insight as a result of the disclosure.

The use of anecdote is probably the closest we ever come to simply defining wisdom through personal experience. We are tapping directly into the lessons that we have learned from our past. We are letting others know that we have been around, that we have a depth of experience and that we can provide insights into their current confusion.

A colleague of mine, Wendy, once described the power of personal anecdote when she recalled the funeral of her mother, who had died when Wendy was only eighteen years old. As the family lined up to shake hands with other mourners at the church, she received a steady stream of well-intended advice around how to cope.

But among all of the simple homilies offered to her, the one phrase that stood out to Wendy was from an elderly aunt who simply looked her in the eye and quietly said, 'I lost my mother at the age of eighteen, too'.

Of all the comments received, from expressed compassion to wise advice and words of comfort, it was this simple self-disclosure that resonated most deeply with Wendy's sadness. *'I know how it feels … I've been there'* is one of the most powerful disclosures we can make. You are speaking from a position of unshakable self-knowledge. There is an inherent wisdom in your words.

Interestingly, when we share anecdotal stories derived from other people we are usually sharing facts rather than wise concepts. While the facts might seem superficially pedantic or trivial, the anecdote actually serves a broader function as it removes us from the here and now, and offers a bigger picture to the discussion. We can extract the wisdom from the parallel themes.

We often start with the phrase 'I met this person once who …' In continuing it is vitally important that we keep the anecdote brief and that we don't distract away from the shared conversational path. We should make sure that the key message is given succinctly at the end, rather like the punchline to a joke. The story should climb inevitably towards the insight.

Something exciting always happens when people get lost

I once had the pleasure of hosting Judith Beck, a globally respected cognitive therapist, when she came to New Zealand to give a two-day workshop. She is a thoroughly nice person, unrelentingly courteous and positive in outlook. After a hugely successful visit, it was time for her to leave.

I drove her to the airport and checked in her bags. There were still 45 minutes before boarding, so I offered to take her for a quick drive to a local scenic lookout point. Thirty minutes later as I drove her back through a maze of unrecognisable streets, I turned to her and confessed, 'Judith, I'm so sorry, but I'm afraid that we're totally lost!'

Her flight to Australia and the rest of her world tour left in just 15 minutes. I was fraught with despair and I expected a furious reply. Instead, I was stunned by her answer. 'Never mind,' she said calmly. 'Something exciting always happens when people get lost! Let's just see what unfolds.'

The world's leading expert in positive thinking had come through with flying colours. In the face of adversity she had kept a steady perspective and handled the situation with exceptional grace.

Judith did catch the plane in time and as I watched her fly away I felt an extraordinary sense of privilege. In the heat of the moment I had learned something quite profound about managing personal tension.

I've told this personal anecdote many times, and apart from name dropping with the central character, it serves wonderfully as a perfect real-life example of the motto, 'Keep Calm and

Carry On'. A catastrophic situation is only as stressful as you choose for it to be!

Something interesting always happens when people get lost …

And finally, before we leave the topic of personal anecdote, we should heed an obvious warning about the excessive use of personal anecdote in conversation — it can bore the pants off your listener if they are not primed or willing to listen!

Using aphorisms, maxims and proverbs

Aphorisms or idioms are succinct phrases in common usage that capture a general truth. They are usually the thoughtful sayings of famous people. For example, 'There's no fool like an old fool'. However, this particular truth has been around for so long that its origins have been lost!

Tired, overused or trite aphorisms are called *clichés*. Clichés are widely accepted truths that have somehow lost their ability to impress or add value to a conversation. An old cliché will rarely provide a moment of insight for the listener, regardless of the inherent wisdom that it still might carry. Everyone gets bored with clichés, almost by definition.

More useful types of aphorisms are called *maxims*, where the emphasis is on providing an apparently 'scientific' truth. The intent is to describe a general rule or guiding principle in life. An example might be 'Lying is always wrong' (Immanuel Kant). Despite the conviction with which this rule might be expressed, it is still not a universal truth and is subject to endless philosophical analysis. It still carries the same subjective quality as all aphorisms, and we tend to choose and express the maxims that suit us best at the time.

The other major class of aphorism that we hear colloquially is called *proverbs*. Here, concrete, commonsense sayings are shared, often based on practical scenarios from everyday life. They tend to be far less expansive in their style, but they still capture the 'aha'. They are very similar to metaphors in that they invite a conceptual leap to a parallel situation.

Common examples might be:

- Make hay while the sun shines.
- Don't cry over spilt milk.
- People who live in glass houses shouldn't throw stones.

These sayings all carry an inherent sense of wisdom. If you are recovering from a relationship break-up and a friend says, 'It's no use crying over spilt milk', then you may well experience a sudden awareness of the futility of your tears and decide to adopt a less sorrowful world view. You may decide to just mop it all up and get on with your life.

Alternatively, you might hear a friend saying that 'Grief is the price that you pay for love', which gives a silver lining to the deep pain that you are feeling. Instead of being lost in your upset, you now see yourself as part of a larger process where the emotional highs have their inevitable downsides later on.

Of course, we must also remember that not everyone appreciates a smug-faced friend hovering around them spouting wise proverbs! We need to choose our moments carefully.

The important question in this section is to ask what proverbs are important to *you*. Which proverbs do you find yourself sharing with others or nodding your head in agreement with?

Proverbs are in use everywhere. If you were to switch on the television, within a 30-minute period you would have heard half a dozen proverbs that you will probably have heard many times before. Characters in soap operas, sound bites from politicians, or interviews with sports coaches after a game … all will tend to use proverbs to get their message across succinctly.

Usually, it makes them seem wise and we admire their ability to put a comforting framework over a confusing event. At other times it seems that they are simply using a tired cliché that lacks genuine authenticity.

As we become increasingly comfortable with quoting proverbs, we develop a more imaginative overview of situations. We jump to spot key themes and can provide succinct commentary that adds insight. In short, we become wise.

My favourite proverbs

Find a list of common proverbs and write down the five that resonate most strongly with you.

1. _____

_____

2. _____

_____

3. _____

_____

4. _____

_____

5. _____

_____

These are time-honoured expressions of wisdom, and by endorsing them, they become *your* wise words. They help you navigate an authentic passage through life and they help you make sense of the turbulence.

Try to slip at least one of them into your conversation before the day has passed. Deliver the words earnestly and with style, and then pause for maximum dramatic effect.

You may be interested to observe the response of your listener!

Knowing our favourite proverbs helps us to know ourselves better. Developing the ability to reference proverbs appropriately in conversation adds colour to our interpersonal style. Proverbs will inevitably lift the conversation from the matter in hand and invite participants to consider the bigger picture. They extract the key issues from the specific facts. We often precipitate 'aha' moments in this way and, more importantly, we often make people smile.

There can be great comfort in realising that old familiar patterns are playing out in our lives. To realise that we are not the first to feel like this, and that we will not be the last. Aphorisms, whether maxims or proverbs, all help lay a reassuring blanket over often painful situations, and can bring a sense of coherence to us in confusing times.

They become an integral part of our world view.

Lawrie's favourite proverb

I once asked my old school friend Lawrie to name his favourite proverb, the one that guides him most reassuringly through life. After the briefest of pauses, he replied, 'Early to bed and early to rise makes Jack a dull boy!'

Lawrie's adolescent humour clearly continued to shine. By cleverly mixing two universally accepted truths, and thinking outside the square, he had created a new truth of his own, and one that reflected his personal world view — and probably mine — with alarming accuracy! (See Chapter Six for more about finding wisdom through humour.)

Pictures that resonate

Pictures can tell a thousand stories. We will all see something slightly different in a picture or image, and often this will reflect issues that we carry within ourselves. Describing what we see in a photograph can reveal an awful lot about us as individuals. We articulate ideas that often we didn't know we had.

On team-building retreats, I will sometimes ask team members to select a picture from a range of randomly photographed images spread across the floor. I ask them to select a photo of how their team looks *currently*, and then another that represents how they would like the team to be *in the future*. They are then asked to describe their pictures to the rest of the group.

The photos may be of cyclists racing, vegetables arranged neatly in boxes, trees in a forest or a hamster on a treadmill. Others show a sunset, a beach, a rock-climber or a pair of tiger cubs playfully pawing at each other. There are 70 images in all, each portraying a different situation.

Initially, participants tend to feel awkward about the exercise and are somewhat reluctant starters. However, as they wander around choosing their pictures, their resistance invariably dissipates and a silence falls over the room. The group becomes deeply reflective and people often spend much longer than I'd planned on choosing their images.

The magic of the exercise occurs when each participant is then asked to describe their photos to the rest of the group. Frequently, one person's image of their *current reality* is chosen by someone else as the image of their *future dream*. It is impossible to predict what photos people will choose and what they will read into them.

For example, someone might choose the hamster in a wheel, describing their work life as mind-numbingly out of their control, and then choose the rock-climber to describe how they want to be. They describe feeling the thrill of the challenging ascent with a clear goal ahead.

Another team member might choose the same images but in precisely the opposite context, feeling terrified about the insecurity of the current situation, perilously clinging to the rock, but looking forward to the structure and security of the purring hamster wheel.

Regardless of the images chosen, as team members talk to their pictures they become increasingly insightful, capturing aspects of their work environment that couldn't be otherwise expressed. I capture the key words as we go and this becomes a powerful basis for subsequent group discussion. Collectively, they will have generated a summary of the present issues facing the team, as well as suggesting a clear vision of how their shared future might look.

We might contrast a *mind-numbing, terrifying and 'out-of-control'* present with the future vision of a *secure, structured and thrilling challenge, with a clear goal* ahead.

These insightful contributions are often made by individuals who are not particularly articulate. They are uncomfortable expressing feelings and opinions, especially in front of their colleagues.

This is what makes the exercise so surprisingly effective. By letting go of the left-brain verbal/logical/critical analysis, and all of the inhibitions that go along with that, we can instead access some surprising right-hemisphere insights, simply through describing pictures to each other.

This, of course, is the inherent magic of appreciating good artwork. It's not necessarily the content of the work that is important; it's what it means to the viewer that counts.

Behind closed doors

I have a painting on the wall of my office of a stick-figure man arriving home from work. He is standing still in the doorway. His wife is rushing towards him, away from an ironing board and an oven. They both have their arms outstretched, but there is a huge space between them on the canvas. She is in the middle of the canvas, and he is appearing from the right-hand side. They both have shadows thrown from a light somewhere behind the man.

The painting is quite striking, black stick figures on a red background, and many people are drawn to it and comment before they sit down while I make them a cup of tea.

For some, the woman seems to be fleeing the domestic chores, with the man as her saviour. For others, the space between them is unbearably large. For others, the shadows suggest a primary energy source located outside of the frame. And for some of my clients, the man seems to be stuck helplessly between the woman's energy and the outside world.

As people speak casually to me about what they see, I notice that they are telling me a lot about themselves. If I was a psychoanalyst interested in projection, I would have more than enough material for a lengthy therapy session even before we had begun!

But as someone who is professionally interested in eliciting insight from others, I could take this opportunity to ask a speculative second question: 'How would you capture the scene in a simple sentence?'

There will be the predictable pause and a sigh, followed by a succinct commentary about some aspect of domestic relationships — often a profoundly thoughtful moment of insight for us both to savour.

Asking what artwork 'means' is a rich source of insight and self-awareness. We are much the wiser for having taken the time to pose the question, not just to other people but also to ourselves.

Your dreams

Is there anything to be learned about ourselves from reviewing the role of our dreams? While I am stopping far short of ever trying to interpret the meaning of a dream, the process of dreaming nonetheless provides a great opportunity for our minds to dwell expansively on big-picture questions.

When we dream, our minds are clearly untethered and free to float off to creative places. The jumbled connections of daytime thoughts and images become woven into an often disturbing story. Just why, or how, is not the question here. Instead, we can simply consider the narratives from recent dreams, and reflect on what insights might be gained from them.

Repeated dreams of falling might suggest that we need to take more control in our lives. Or if we dream of running naked through public places, desperately looking for a hiding place, then we might decide that we need to stand tall and be proud of who we are inside. Everyone will come to their own conclusions about what is to be learned from a dream. We don't need expert analysis; it's just more material from 'out of the box' that can provide us with insight.

It is of interest to note that good questions that ask about *meaning* are the key technique for eliciting self-wisdom, rather than the actual content of a dream. Simply recounting a weird dream is one thing; looking for meaning is quite another.

My favourite dream

- Write down a brief synopsis of your favourite dream. _____

  _____

  _____

  _____

  _____

- What does it tell us about you? What are the key insights to be gained? _____

  _____

  _____

  _____

Summary

There are many colourful ways in which we can capture and share personal insights in our lives. Opportunities occur for us throughout everyday life to gain clarity and wisdom about both ourselves and the world around us.

Everyday language is full of rich wisdom. Proverbs, maxims and popular quotes can all add value to our catalogue of simple truths. Similarly, we can also find insight in creative artwork that we admire. Even our dreams can provide us with 'aha' moments if we bother to reflect on them properly.

The on-going quest for personal insight never ends and the inherent curiosity involved in the search can feel very life-affirming. It has been said that when we stop looking for insight, we are not truly living, we are simply surviving. And we can all do better than that.

Chapter Five

CLEVER CONVERSATIONS WITH OTHERS

There are at least three common situations where the ability to lift a conversation can add value; interactions where we can extract wisdom from others and where our world becomes personally richer as a result.

Firstly, we shall look at how to enrich those boring conversations that are based simply on a stream of facts. Secondly, we shall consider how best to extract wisdom from children. And finally, we shall learn how to draw out wisdom from the elderly.

How to enrich a tedious conversation

Have you ever found yourself locked into a conversation which seems purely mundane? For example, a friend giving you a blow-by-blow account of a movie they've just seen? Or a partner reporting word for word what they did during the day? Or a pedantic neighbour telling you exactly how you should live your life?

These are all boring conversations that grind along at a pedestrian level. They are simple streams of facts broadcast monotonously where the intention is to inform rather than to delight. They are sharing knowledge and information, but they are not inducing wisdom. In short, they aren't particularly clever or stimulating conversations.

However, the key thing to remember is that regardless of how someone interacts with us, we can always choose our response. We can choose to respond by asking a second question, and we can look to extract genuine nuggets of wisdom from the truckloads of earthy facts offered. By asking clever questions, we can encourage others to think a little more expansively about the way they see life.

There's more than one way to cut a cake

A few years ago I was stuck in an airport shuttle bus with a group of young mothers heading out for a fun weekend away. They were all excited and were talking endlessly about their children, recipes, home appliances and clothes. I was so bored!

The conversation turned to children's birthday parties. Factual information continued to be exchanged. And then, out of the blue, just as someone had noted how hard it is to cut a cake into five pieces, one of the quieter mothers dropped a stunning second question into the mix.

She simply asked, 'What is the most important thing to take into account when you're cutting up a cake?'

Suddenly the whole tone of the conversation changed. There was the classic reflective pause before everyone began discussing life at a far deeper level. Should we cut the cake into equal portions? Or according to need? Or cut size according to the most deserving? Or to the most polite? Should we decide on their behalf or should we ask them first?

In seconds, it seemed like I was sitting in a university undergraduate politics or philosophy seminar. We had been collectively transported to a higher plane of analysis by one simple question. *Suddenly, the cake seemed to have become a perfect metaphor for life.*

We were addressing basic principles of how to share limited resources and each was expressing strong and deeply held personal beliefs. The conversation seemed to fly from that point, subsequently moving on to consider a range of fundamental lessons that we as parents teach kids about life.

And so it went on. By the end of the trip, I was no longer bored. I was inspired!

When people talk excessively about an event in a factual way, they are not bringing the story to a conclusion. The reasons for the stream of factual details are not clear. Somehow, we need to encourage the storyteller to jump to the essential message.

A classic way of drawing out meaning from the monologue is to interrupt politely by asking, '… and what is the moral of the story?'

You are expressing interest and seeking clarification in the style of curiosity as described in Chapter Three, but you are also requiring the answer to be pitched at a conceptual level. There will be a necessary pause while the bigger picture is considered before the key message is revealed.

We don't need to become frustrated or irritable to bring a long-winded story to a close. An abrupt interjection isn't necessary. Instead, we can recognise the situation that we are in and look within ourselves for a good question to lift up the conversation. We can extract the key points from the story and we can transform the stream of facts into a genuine opportunity for insight.

When people are talking at you they are usually trying to share an experience that has somehow touched them. By asking good questions you can help them to frame up the exchange so that you can also be touched and perhaps even inspired by the same events.

You can help them to find the essential message that they wish to share.

Wisdom from children

Talking to children is brilliant. They are delightfully uninhibited and they will use all kinds of expressive techniques to get their point across. They often surprise us with their unique take on life.

Some years ago, my daughter Jessica, then aged seven, was asked by her teacher what her father did for a living.

'He's a psychologist,' she replied.

'And what does a psychologist do?' the teacher asked.

'He makes sad people happy … like a clown,' was the acutely perceptive reply.

What more could I possibly say? There it was in black and white. My daughter thought I was a clown!

It is often said that 'out of the mouths of fools and children comes great wisdom'. But many of us find it hard to communicate with children and we struggle to find the right things to ask.

How often, on their children's return from school, do parents ask, 'How was your day?' To be met with a gruff reply, 'All right.'

Or 'What did you do today?' And the reply, 'Nothing.'

The quest for facts is fatally doomed and will never lead to a satisfying conversation. Instead, it is far, far better to lure children into replying to a second question, and then marvelling at the depth of their appreciation of the world.

Goldfish wisdom

Once, when wandering around an English stately home, I was drawn to a lily pond full of large goldfish. Two young children were gazing deeply into the pool.

'What do you think about when you look at goldfish?' I casually asked.

'I remember my aunty who died,' the young girl replied. 'She kept goldfish in a bowl and always told me that because they were surrounded by water, they never knew it was there. She said it was like happiness ... it's all around us, if only we realised it.'

And then she skipped away, leaving me mouthing noiselessly in goldfish land! It had been such a simple question, and it had elicited such a wise reply.

Children love fantasy, they love play and they love magic. All can be used to generate thoughtful ideas. As parents or as significant adults it is important that, as we play or read to children, we also ask questions to encourage them to be more expansive in their outlook.

The magical world that kids love to visit is a particularly good theatre for asking extraordinary questions to draw wisdom from kids. Often you can set up the most outrageous of scenarios to extract surprising ideas. Fancy dress, imaginative paintings, playing on the beach ... all of these situations set the scene for great conversations.

As you build the sandcastle, you can muse about life in the olden days. You can ask imaginative questions as you play.

'What would be the most important thing to do if you lived in a castle? Why?'

'Who would you need to be with you? Why?'

Play therapy, art therapy and music therapy all have childlike connotations where we can regress into the dreamy world of imagination and fantasy. We can be what we want, do what we want and invent what we want.

It's a wonderful world where anything goes and as we construct our dreams we can discover much about ourselves and each other. Children are comfortable in that place where most adults are not. They love to speculate, imagine and guess in the land of the unknown.

But they have to pause, reflect and capture the key messages to become wise. The questions need to be asked, or the moment slips by as just another amusing game.

Most collections of childhood stories such as the tales of Hans Christian Andersen, the tales of the Arabian nights or Grimms' fairytales, all lend themselves perfectly to brief conversations afterwards. It's a great opportunity to lift up from a simple story and invite bigger picture thinking.

- What does that story remind you of?
- What was the best bit for you? Why?
- If you told that story to a friend, what might they think?

Sadly, we usually use these bedtime stories simply to encourage children to nod off to sleep and the opportunity for a thoughtful de-brief is lost.

My favourite children's story

Think back to your early childhood and recall your favourite fairytale or story. If you are a parent, or still read stories to children, think about what story you most enjoy reading and have the greatest empathy for. Write it down.

My favourite story is:_____

_____

_____

_____

_____

_____

What is the story's key message about life?_____

_____

_____

_____

_____

_____

Some of the more endearing comments made by small children when interviewed on television are usually the direct result of the questions asked. For example, asking: 'What do you want for Christmas?' will elicit a simple list of demands.

Conversely, asking 'How do you think Father Christmas gets down the chimney?' will open up a free-thinking and imaginative range of potential answers.

Children are creative, imaginative and are not constrained by practical considerations. They will come up with the most wonderfully inventive solutions to a challenging question and will happily share their colourful ideas with you. To gain maximum value for you both, you need to be equally inventive and lead the conversation forward with your unrelenting curiosity to hear more.

Five creative questions to ask a child

I asked my good friends Graham and Cynthia, who have been teaching primary school children for many years, what the five most creative questions were to ask a child. They paused, went away to think about it, and returned with the following suggestions.

1. If you had a time machine and went far into the future, what would be different?
2. How would you like the future to be?
3. If you were an animal, what sort would you be? What would you tell humans?
4. If you could design a city in the future, what would it look like?
5. What has been your biggest mistake? How could you fix it?

We can all ask our own variations of these simple questions. If we give ourselves a creative stretch by choosing expansive questions, we are usually rewarded by the creativity of the reply.

Another important factor to consider when talking with children is to realise that the world is changing fast. Faster than ever before. And at the same time, many time-honoured truths about life are falling by the wayside. Children now live in a digital world of screens and online connectivity. Much of the wisdom of the past no longer has relevance to them. 'Buy now, pay later' today seems to be a smarter way of living rather than the previous sage advice about 'saving for a rainy day'.

Values such as loyalty and commitment have also faded away noticeably. In their place, a more immediate, self-indulgent world view predominates, with a more disposable attitude to both material commodities and also to relationships. These are not necessarily bad changes, but they are certainly different perspectives on life and they bring a different set of values to the table.

When acknowledged, these differences can become the very stuff of a rich and rewarding conversation with the young. When they are not acknowledged, they become severe impediments to an engaging discussion.

It is best to treat children as if they speak a different language and come from a different culture. Assume nothing, maintain a careful respect and tread carefully. They are more intellectually agile than you — and they can also bite!

Their wisdom is different and it's delightful.

Wisdom from the elderly

Visiting the elderly can be a torturous affair filled with long awkward pauses while trivial details of the day are reviewed. 'How are you keeping?', 'What did you have for lunch?', and 'How's the weather been recently?' would all be typical questions for us to ask. They are present-focused, factual and objective. Sadly, by carrying on in this way, we are not mining for the incredible depth of wisdom that each and every older person has to share with us.

Every older person has a deep well of experience to draw on when expressing themselves. In their advancing years they become more reflective and they tend to integrate their key understandings about the world. They can use small anecdotes to wonderful effect and will often relay simple truths about life with great authenticity. In general, the older you are, the wiser you become.

Entering into conversation with an older person becomes so much more fulfilling when you adopt a healthy curiosity towards their general view on life. Just as Dr Foster was curious about the lessons I had learned over my clinical career, so too should we be interested to hear what the elderly have to say. Their subjective world view will often bring a surprisingly fresh perspective to almost any situation.

Older people are typically more reserved in their interpersonal style, adopting the role of 'detached observer' with a natural ease. Their race is almost run, but they are still watching from the sidelines with a perspective born of many years' experience. They've seen it all before and they can look at the present situation through the frame of history. It's all swings and roundabouts. The pendulum swings. And what goes around comes around. The more things change, the more things stay the same.

We can tap into this 'passive bystander' perspective by asking good questions; not to elicit fixed opinions about how the world should be, but to establish considered truths about the patterns that they see in life. Older people naturally tend to pull back and see the wider context. They can see 'meaning' and they can see reasons why things happen in a way that the main players on today's stage cannot. It's a simple tactic for us to simply ask them:

- What does this all mean to you?
- What would you have made of this when you were that age?
- How does it differ these days?

Life really isn't so hard to understand and the older we get, the simpler things seem. Older people can cut through to basic truths in a way that more energised, youthful characters struggle to do. Most of us are so caught up in the business of living that we cannot step back and 'see the wood for the trees'.

Conversely, the elderly stand back and place themselves outside the game. They are astute observers of life as it all unfolds around them. They are usually delighted to be asked to extract the key learnings from what they have seen over the grand sweep of their lives.

One of the greatest gifts that you can give an older person is to listen to their wisdom. If you ask the right questions, they will offer you the greatest gifts in return: the gift of their insights, their wisdom and their experience.

Considering one's personal answers to second questions is what later life is all about. Old age gives us the time and the opportunity to step back and reflect. But if we let that opportunity slip by, then we simply drift through our final days until we pass on and our impact on others is diminished.

As life draws towards its inevitable conclusion, there is a huge satisfaction to be gained in summarising and drawing together our personal conclusions from everything we have seen and heard. Over all of the years that the elderly have lived, they have experienced a great deal. They have learned from the tough times, they have learned from the good. They have usually made some mistakes, but they have also worked out the basic principles by which they have lived out their lives and stayed true to what they believe in.

Old age is a time of life when we can all decide what might be written about us on a metaphorical headstone or spoken about us in a eulogy.

In his book *ACT Made Simple: An easy to read primer on Acceptance and Commitment Therapy,* Russ Harris proposes a string of brilliant questions that might be asked of us as we approach the end of our lives:

- What do you really stand for in life?
- What really matters, deep in your heart?
- What do you want to be remembered for at your funeral?
- What were your heart's deepest desires, for whom you wanted to be and for what you wanted to do during your brief time on this planet?

It may seem a little gloomy to be considering such matters, but these are important questions to ask. The answers may only be simple, somewhat trite, phrases, but they will give enormous access to the wisdom of an elderly person. It becomes their gift to the rest of us. It becomes our received wisdom.

We all can have the privilege of leaving a deep and meaningful legacy. All that is required is for those around us to ask us the right questions and for them to skilfully elicit our final grand message to the world.

Summary

We have looked at how we might enrich conversations that otherwise sit heavily on our shoulders. With pedantic, rather tedious conversationalists, we can hurry them up by asking good questions. We can help them cut to the chase and find their key message.

With children, we can share their delight in fantasy and magic, drawing out extraordinarily insightful comments by probing with the right questions. They will continually delight and surprise us.

And finally, with the elderly, we can reminisce wistfully and identify their key learnings from a deep reservoir of past experience.

Children are excited by looking forward into the magical future, unconstrained by the practicalities of the real world. Conversely, the elderly enjoy looking back, drawing on their wisdom extracted from years of experience.

The key message from this chapter, however, is that we can all become more tactically astute when talking with others. We can lift up the conversation, and we can communicate with others on a different level. We can elicit wise words from anyone we choose to ask, and we can learn so much from them as a consequence.

Chapter Six

WISDOM RECEIVED FROM OTHERS

The most common 'aha' experience in life is when we hear a simple, time-honoured phrase that helps us frame our world view. We often trade the 'received wisdom' of philosophers and social commentators who have gone before. Examples might include well-known individuals such as Confucius, Plato and Shakespeare. Their legacy lives on in their words, hundreds of years after they have died. They had the ability to put words together so eloquently that nothing more needs to be said. They have captured an idea perfectly.

Many of their phrases have since fallen into common use, and we now find ourselves referencing them with ease, often not realising where they originally came from. This is perhaps the greatest achievement of a wise person: for their ideas to live on in the minds and language of all who follow.

In addition to such broadly accepted wisdom that is embedded in our culture, we also receive more specific ideas from those closer to us. We learn phrases and everyday sayings from our parents, our role models and our favourite media stars that help to guide our passage through the world. We often don't realise that these phrases or sayings are not universally true, but we take them on board as facts, or commonsense rules, by which to live our lives.

For some of us, 'Life is what you make it'. For others, 'Whatever happens, happens'. These are two simple and equally valid truths, but they set up very different perspectives on life and the way that we live it.

It is important to note from the outset that for every succinct one-liner that was ever written, there will undoubtedly be a counter truth that others hold equally dear to their hearts! Einstein once wrote that 'common sense is the collection of prejudices acquired by age eighteen'.

In this chapter we will be reviewing the main sources of received wisdom in our lives and then we will pause to reflect on the key messages that we have taken on board from each of them.

Insights from your elders

As we travel through life we all have the privilege of sharing the journey at different times with wise people. They are experienced, thoughtful characters and they are prepared to share their wisdom with us. Sometimes they occupy formal roles in our development. Teachers and parents would be typical examples. Others might have more specific roles, such as sports coaches and youth camp leaders.

Some are there for the whole journey, while others have a more transient role. Each has their place in mentoring us and helping us see the bigger picture.

We frequently meet up with fellow travellers on the road of life who simply seem wise, and from whom we can learn a great deal.

They may be classmates, flatmates or team mates. They are usually individuals who demonstrate a maturity beyond their years. They provide fleeting connections with us that leave a strong impression. For example, we might receive a casual comment from someone passing us on the street or standing in a queue. It can seem so perceptive that it will stop us dead in our tracks.

Insights can be found anywhere and they can be surprisingly profound.

In the left-hand column, write down the names of five people who have been the most instrumental in shaping your life. Against their names, write down an inspirational sentence that captures their key message to you about living life well.

The key influences in my life	Their simple message to me about 'living life well'

Insight from your role models

In childhood and beyond, we adopt heroes and role models whom we admire. We do not usually know them personally, but they embody all that we value in life. They may have achieved great things, they may have extraordinary talents, or they may have qualities that we wish we could share.

Our own aspirations are reflected in the lives of those whom we admire. It is interesting to pause and reflect on who our heroes have been over the years. They will be individuals whose lives have served as an inspiration to us, and whose values we share. Often they are remembered for one or two specific quotes about life, and for one or two brief anecdotal events that subsequently attain legendary significance.

Think of Martin Luther King Jr: 'I have a dream.'

Think of John Lennon: 'Life is what happens when you're busy making other plans.'

Think of Neil Armstrong: 'That's one small step for a man ... one giant leap for mankind.'

We remember Martin Luther King Jr leading civil rights marches. We remember John Lennon with Yoko, lying in bed for peace. We remember Neil Armstrong descending the ladder from the space capsule.

Our heroes have their time-honoured quotes and images. When an athlete stands triumphantly upon the podium, the next thing that they say is invariably taken as a wonderfully insightful gift to the rest of us. They may seem humble, arrogant or driven. And their gift to the world will invariably have been prompted by a second question asked by the media.

As they bask in the glory of their triumph, they will often be asked 'What was the secret to your success?' There will be a pause, a thoughtful moment for reflection and then the profound insight will be revealed.

Ironically, when Sir Edmund Hillary came down from being the first man to climb Mount Everest, the question wasn't properly asked. He is now immortalised as simply saying 'Well, we knocked the bastard off!' Hardly an insightful comment but still memorable, as it enshrines the simple humility of the man at the moment of his greatest triumph.

Five significant role models in my life

Think back over your life and write down the names of five individuals who have been key role models for you. They could be sports stars, musicians, politicians or movie stars. Then, in the right-hand column, write down one wise 'gift' from them in terms of how to live life well.

My significant role models	Their inspirational quotes

Prescribed insights from popular sources

Any bookshop will have a range of small inspirational books carrying brief reflections and quotes. Most newspapers will also publish a thought for the day. Daily spiritual devotions or one-line messages displayed on billboards outside churches all offer simple truths to reflect upon. The world is full of opportunities to have an 'aha' moment inspired by the wisdom of others.

More formal collections of quotes (such as *Webster's Pocket Quotation Dictionary* or *The Oxford Dictionary of Quotations*) can provide a rich source of inspirational insights into life. Flicking through these reference books and picking out your favourite sayings can be a great way to spend a rainy afternoon.

As we saw in Chapter One, many wise, thoughtful sayings prevail around funerals, loss and grief. A whole industry of insightful one-liners has evolved around these poignant moments in life's journey. They are moments when people stop to reflect on their journey. They are moments when we appreciate a few well-chosen lines on a greetings card.

Similarly, marriage celebrants are full of prescriptive quotes that advise the couple, and also remind the assembled witnesses, of the key ingredients that make up a happy marriage. Their popular quotes become our personal truths. They become the rock-solid foundations for our perceptions of the world.

The social currency of insight

A friend once told me how he had developed a great idea of writing simple phrases or proverbs on bank notes. He carried an indelible marker pen and would sit in a coffee bar writing wise sayings on any banknotes that came to hand. It was his party trick when in company.

He would enjoy writing things such as 'The best things in life are free' or 'You reap what you sow' on ten-dollar notes. He would imagine the reaction of anyone who received it later. Their emotion would probably be best defined as puzzled delight.

In his own way my friend was freely sharing wisdom and

simple truths. He was adding value to all subsequent financial exchanges.

However, it turned out later that technically he was defacing the currency and it was a criminal offence. So please do not be inspired to follow in his example — treat it as a witty anecdote!

Insights from the internet

The virtual world of internet search engines can provide easy access to websites that offer simple, insightful quotes. We can now search for all kinds of wisdom on the internet and opportunities have opened up dramatically for us to access big picture ideas.

An example might be the TED talks website (ww.ted.com) that provides a rich source of insightful thoughts for the day. TED talks (Technology, Entertainment and Design) are provided by a global, non-profit organisation dedicated to promoting 'ideas worth spreading'. They offer 'riveting talks by remarkable people'. A TED talk will typically last 20 minutes or so, and will usually provide a succinct summary at the end. But even if the insights aren't handed to you on a platter, it is still easy to take a few minutes after the conclusion of a talk to ask yourself what the key messages have been. A TED talk of whatever persuasion tends to be full of metaphor, inspiring ideas and provides delightful approaches to life. They are free and accessible to all.

Another great opportunity provided by the internet is to follow certain individuals on Twitter, or to follow people who blog. It is worthwhile choosing to follow one or two philosophical, spiritual or intellectual bloggers, and to receive their insights on a daily basis. Deepak Chopra, His Holiness the Dalai Lama, and Stephen Hawking can all offer us regular 'aha' moments in this most accessible of ways.

Insights from literature/the arts

Tell me what you read, and I'll tell you who you are.

François Mauriac

Most great works of literature and stage plays provide fantastic quotes that have fallen into popular use. They also capture themes and dramatic truths about life that we can strongly identify with. Most people will be able to name their favourite book relatively easily, but following this up with the second question 'Why?' will almost certainly give rise to more deliberate rumination.

We rarely stop to think about what appeals to us about our favourite books or authors. Sometimes it might be the author's style (witty, dry, ironic or sensitive). It might be the type of storyline (a thriller, a romance or a mystery). Or it might be the emotional tone that is set. Invariably we identify strongly with the world view of the central character.

In terms of finding simple truths about life from literature, we probably need go no further than William Shakespeare to see how powerful the written word can be. His succinct observations have seeped into all aspects of contemporary life. We all quote his wise words frequently, often without realising it. For a playwright who died over 400 years ago, Shakespeare has left a remarkable impact on us all. For example, on one page of *Hamlet* (Act I Scene III) he scripts Polonius's advice to Laertes. This brief speech contains twenty lines of quotable wisdom, and the marvel is that some 400 years later, we probably hear some aspect of the wise messages repeated on most days! Some of the most popular quotes include:

- 'Give thy thoughts no tongue.'
- 'Give every man thine ear, but few thy voice.'

- 'Neither a borrower nor a lender be.'

- And famously, 'To thy own self be true.'

All of these nuggety truths are powerful examples of received wisdom from literature.It is no accident that conceptually we think of libraries and books as the central repository for wisdom. The central storehouse of knowledge for a civilisation is generally considered to be found in its libraries and its books. Libraries represent the accumulated wisdom of many generations over many years. Literature still holds the key for our collective database for wisdom.

Insights from poetry

Poetry is a form of writing that has a particularly strong ability to capture wisdom in a few simple words. Its strength is in the succinct phrasing and poignant themes. All successful poetry will capture an idea or offer meaningful insight in just a few words. The poet's art is to connect with us and to provide a delightful message of wisdom to be shared.

A great example of a widely-quoted poem that speaks profoundly for many of us is *If*, written by Rudyard Kipling in the late nineteenth century. Among the better known lines are:

> *If you can keep your head while all around*
> *Are losing theirs and blaming it on you,*
> *If you can trust yourself when all men doubt you,*
> *But make allowance for their doubting too;*
>
> ...
>
> *Yours is the Earth and everything that's in it,*
> *And — which is more — you'll be a Man, my son!*

This poem offers us a series of wonderfully simple truths about how to be a man, or more correctly, how to live life well. It is the gift from an older, wiser man sharing the secrets of how to live a fulfilling life.

Another widely quoted source of wisdom is *Desiderata*, written in 1927 by American writer, Max Ehrmann. It has gained considerable popularity over the intervening years.

> *Go placidly amidst the noise and haste,*
> *and remember what peace there may be in silence.*
> *As far as possible and without surrender*
> *be on good terms with all persons.*
> *Speak your truth quietly and clearly;*
> *and listen to others, even the dull and the ignorant;*
> *they too have their story …*

Again this lengthy text is crammed full of wise advice, very much in the style of Kipling's poem. In each case we are being offered a series of maxims from a wise sage and benefitting from their accumulated life experiences.

There are many classic texts from which we can draw wise advice about how to live a fulfilling life. Their popular phrases go round and around in conversation almost without a thought. We can all pluck our preferred gems of wisdom from this treasure trove of simple truths.

However, we should also acknowledge that there are perceptive insights to be gained from *any* book or poem that we read. Wisdom does not sit exclusively in the writings of the great communicators. If you enjoy a certain type of book or a particular author, then it is hugely rewarding to stop and wonder why you are drawn to them. And what lessons you can learn.

The second of these two questions, as we have seen, will almost certainly open a door to greater self-awareness for you and will add to your catalogue of received wisdom.

Insights from witty one-liners

Another character who is well known for his ability to generate insightful gems of wisdom is Oscar Wilde. Although primarily a playwright whose works contain many quotable lines, he is best remembered for his quick-witted conversational style.

A leading socialite in late nineteenth-century London, Wilde is often characterised as being the centre of attention at fashionable parties, offering his opinion on everything and nothing. He was a flamboyant, narcissistic character, for whom the world was truly a stage. His plays were well known for their incisive commentary on social issues.

Oscar Wilde used his quick wit to cut to the heart of an issue. He made words dance with his clever contributions to a conversation. His witty one-line truths were usually expressed as paradoxical remarks, expressing exactly the opposite of what he meant. These are known as *epigrams*. He is very quotable and it can be a great pleasure to draw on his wisdom at appropriate times.

His more popular lines include:

- 'Experience is simply the name that we give our mistakes.'
- 'Every saint has a past, and every sinner has a future.'
- 'A man who does not think for himself, does not think at all.'
- 'Keep love in your heart. A life without it is like a sunless garden when the flowers are dead.'
- 'I can resist everything except temptation.'
- 'An idea that is not dangerous is unworthy of being called an idea at all.'

The list simply goes on and on. Oscar Wilde was a veritable fountain of wisdom that spilled out into any conversation that involved him. Not for him were the pedantic exchanges of facts or social gossip. He would be able to lift any tedious discussion into the conceptual realm, simply by interjecting with a witty epigram.

So how can we weave Oscar Wilde, or similar wordsmiths, into our lives such that we become wiser as people? Do we have to remember his quotes or study his work in great detail?

If we hear a brilliant line that speaks to us, then we will probably have an 'aha' moment. The flash of the light bulb will briefly illuminate our mind. However, unless we take steps to capture the insight and hold it for ourselves, the moment passes and we are none the wiser on the following day.

Time, perhaps, to run an inventory over our personal warehouse of wisdom and see what we have on the shelves!

Wisdom from literary figures

To establish where you currently sit in these matters it is useful to answer the following questions. You may struggle to come up with definitive answers to these questions immediately, but if you take the time to reflect, and maybe research a little, you will be generously rewarded.

- Which literary figures do you commonly quote? _____

  _____

  _____

- What are your favourite lines from literature or the arts? _____

  _____

  _____

- Of all the lines that Shakespeare wrote, what would be your favourite? _____

  _____

  _____

- And finally, to give the exercise an extra edge, you might ask yourself a quick 'second question': *Why* are these my favourite quotes? _____

  _____

  _____

  _____

  _____

Insights from the visual arts

How can a painter apply a few brushstrokes of paint onto a blank canvas and create a masterpiece that remains inspirational for hundreds of years? What is it that allows artists to capture a moment in freeze frame and take our breath away? Paintings, photographs and simple sketches all have an amazing ability to inspire and speak wisely to us. The visual arts provide us with a great window onto life far beyond the here and now.

If we read any informed commentary about a particular piece of artwork, we will inevitably hear how an image has astutely captured and projected a profoundly insightful truth about some aspect of life.

For example, there are many diverse opinions about the painting of the *Mona Lisa*. Well known for the sitter's enigmatic smile, this painting means different things to different people. For some, it speaks of mystery. She is beautiful, but not in a classic sense. The hands lie limp but firmly in her lap. For others, there is a strong affinity with the background scene, reflecting harmony and connection with nature.

Her identity is not known and the subsequent speculation invites us to wonder who she is, what she thinks, what she feels and what she believes in.

These comments are not simple descriptions of the composition. They are abstract comments that suggest bigger ideas behind the painted image. They invite us to be drawn into the imagery, and to be awakened to a broader appreciation of the work.

The comments could easily be re-framed as second questions, perhaps in an art history exam, where the student is asked:

- What is the key message conveyed by the painting?
- What does her expression seem to suggest?

In our replies to these open-ended invitations, we will reveal far more about our own ideas, values and past experiences than we will ever realise. The questions will extract wisdom from us. Learning to access and discuss artwork, to help decide for ourselves what a particular item represents, is a major technique for accessing personal wisdom. A painting is simply a mirror in which we can thoughtfully observe our reflected ideas.

Insights from music

Music has been described as the soundtrack to our lives. The lyrics, the melodies and the emotional angst remain embedded in our minds for years after we first experienced them. Music has a way of speaking to us, and the songs often capture exactly the personal and social issues of the day. We identify strongly with the accessible messages from popular culture.

For some, it is the joyous trill of a catchy pop song; for others, the overwhelming despair of the blues. The anger of punk or the aching disappointment of country and western music all have a way of cutting right through to the essence of life for each category of fan. Our thoughts about everything that we feel can be captured in the title of a song.

'I'm a country music fan,' speaks volumes about a person. They are telling us more than they realise about themselves. Their hopes, dreams, past experiences and values all become wrapped up in a label.

When we attend a concert, we cannot help but notice the similarity among members of the audience, all drawn to the event to celebrate a style of music, with lyrics that capture the essential message. Comfortable, homely types will converge at a folk festival, while ageing baby boomers will gather at an Eagles concert. Meanwhile, disaffected young rappers will breakdance to hip-hop in the town square. Everyone is tuned in to the collective vibe that defines their particular kind of music. They are all affirming a common message about the world and celebrating the shared insights as expressed by the artists concerned.

As Bob Dylan mournfully wails that 'It's all over now, Baby Blue', thousands of people hold up cigarette lighters in quiet acknowledgement of a simple truth. He is speaking for them and they will later hum the song in the car, sing it in the shower and play it to their friends. Bob's wisdom about separation and loss is being celebrated and passed around by his followers, eagerly looking to share the message with like-minded souls.

Every popular songster has their portfolio of quotable song titles or chorus lines. The Beatles told us that 'money can't buy me love'. Dire Straits assured us that 'there should be sunshine after rain', and The Rolling Stones reminded us that 'you can't always get what you want'. All songs that provide wise words help soothe our souls. Rod Stewart reminded us that 'A nod is as good as a wink to a blind horse', while John Lennon urged us to 'Imagine ...'

The hook phrases of our favourite songs will stay deep in our psyche. They become our anthems and usually remind us of the core values and ideals that drove us in our formative years. In quietly reflective moments, they can make us cry.

We can all find great wisdom in the songs that we hear. Songwriters are the great sages of the twenty-first century.

Wisdom from your favourite songs

In the table below write down the names of your favourite musicians, your favourite song of theirs and what it means to you.

Favourite singers/bands	Most significant song	Key message

Note any common themes or particularly significant truths that resonate profoundly for you. What does your musical taste tell you about your personal take on life? _____

_____

_____

In looking over your list, what themes do you notice about your

choices? _____

_____

_____

What are your musical influences telling us about you? _____

_____

_____

_____

Wisdom from the silver screen

In a similar way to songs, movies can also have a profound effect on our lives. While songs provide instant hooks and tunes to capture an insight, movies tend to build with a slow burn until the powerful 'aha' is revealed at the end. It is worth noting that the most enduringly successful movies will have a catchphrase as their legacy; a phrase or a quote that perfectly captures some aspect of the storyline.

Dorothy in *The Wizard of Oz* tells us that 'there's no place like home'. Ali McGraw in *Love Story* tells us that 'love means never having to say you're sorry'. In *Gone with the Wind*, Scarlett O'Hara reminds us that 'tomorrow is another day'. We can all cite our favourite movies and their memorable scenes. We can usually describe the main story, but can we capture the key messages that the movie has given us? What are the favourite sound bites or images that stay with us forever?

In the box below, list your favourite three movies and try to extract the key messages:

My favourite movies	The most memorable scene/line	Key message

Insights from comedy/cartoons (finding the 'aha' in hahaha)

The quick humour of a comedian is a rich source of pithy wisdom. In a flamboyant moment they can deliver a cutting insight, often using irony or biting sarcasm. The humour invariably comes from de-bunking an established truth, often by championing the opposite truth.

By laughing at the punchline of a joke, we are endorsing the conclusion as a satisfying comment that agrees with us. It is a surprising twist on conventional wisdom and usually provides plenty of food for thought.

As we all know, there has been 'many a true word spoken in jest!' This truism is the defining characteristic of powerful humour. Comedy is not just a superficial silliness, instead it provides an opportunity for us to think more carefully about life and challenges some of the assumptions that we generally make.

It is a huge mistake to view comedy simply as entertainment. There is invariably a strong message embedded in humour, often captured by a simple catchphrase or a clumsy mistake. When we think about who are our favourite comedians, we might consider what their key message to the world could be. By knocking convention or arrogance, for example, they are implicitly promoting innovation and humility. If the jokes are consistently sexist or racist, what is the real message that is being conveyed? Are we joking about it because we believe it or because we don't?

Confusingly, the message in most comedy runs exactly counter to the underlying philosophical position that is being promoted. Often, humour is ironic or cynical. We say exactly the opposite of what we actually mean. We say what we don't mean, in order to ridicule a truth. We are mocking conventional wisdom. We challenge established assumptions about the world.

Who are your favourite comedians/comedy shows?_____

_____

_____

_____

What is their key theme/message? _____

_____

_____

_____

_____

Summary

There are many ways in which we can acquire wisdom and insight from others. This chapter encourages you to reflect upon the key influences in your own life, and the key messages that you have learned from them. The more that we can reference the established wisdom of others in our life, the more likely we are to move on to sparkling new insights of our own.

Chapter Seven

BEING WISE ABOUT
THE WORLD

As we move through life we learn facts and we gain knowledge. Some people become very skilled and know a great deal, but often these very intelligent, learned individuals are not 'worldly wise'. Although they are knowledgeable, they seem to lack a connection or wider appreciation of the real world. They have learned a lot, but they have not developed wisdom through their experiences.

Most of the examples of wisdom that have been used so far are simple truths about the world in general. We often use sayings that seem to apply generally to people's lives, such as 'What goes around comes around' or 'The best things in life are free'. These simple truths help us to make sense of how the world works. We genuinely believe them.

Although they initially seem to be objective facts, they are not scientifically proven truths. They are simply observations about general patterns in life, based on an individual's personal and selective review of their past experiences. And if we stop to think for a moment, often what goes around *doesn't* come around! And some of the best things in life *do* cost money!

Other people may adopt phrases or sayings that promote exactly the opposite world view. Some may say that 'history never repeats itself' or 'you only get what you pay for in life'.

For every simple truth, there are usually perfectly plausible alternative truths that other individuals might use that promote a completely different perspective on the world.

Let's consider what simple truths seem most important to us personally in explaining how the world operates. In doing so we can identify the key principles that we endorse and perhaps wish to broadcast to others. Every time that you say, 'life is all about relationships' or 'life is all about fairness', you are making a political statement. You are promoting a particular world view that you wish to affirm.

For some people, life 'is all about being kind to one another'. They will say this when watching TV, hearing of a friend's problems or in the heat of an argument. To them, it's a simple truth, and to them, kindness is the paramount aspect of a life well lived.

If you believe a simple truth to be true, then you should probably be actively campaigning for others to share it with you. Your worldly wisdom is the generic wisdom that you have to offer others and they may then increasingly seek out comments and observations from you.

So how do we capture our truths about the world? How do we know which core beliefs make us 'wise'? The answer, of course, is to reflect and to take the time to identify phrases and sayings that we commonly use. Some people can do this easily and possibly spend too much of their time offering gems of wisdom to others. But for most of us, the skill of capturing a moment by extracting the key message in a sentence is a struggle. It is a skill that we need to practise.

When we have to write a few words in a card, whether it is a birthday celebration or a farewell, we often feel stuck for what to say. We feel the burden of expectation to share something profound, and to write down a few wise words.

'Happy birthday' or 'I'll miss you', can seem a little formulaic in these circumstances. Far better to draw on a reservoir of thoughtful phrases such as 'make every candle count', or 'parting is such sweet sorrow' (Shakespeare again) to share something deeper with your friend.

Every card represents an opportunity to dig a little deeper and share your personal wisdom about life.

Simple observations as potential insights

Probably the easiest form of shared insight is to simply state what you see. This applies especially if your observation is the recognition of a pattern or a general rule. If you listen to the conversation of any interesting person, they invariably share sweeping observations of the world that provide interesting new angles on a familiar subject.

For example, on watching a flock of birds passing, one might remark that 'It's interesting how they all behave as one connected entity. They seem to all be part of a shared consciousness.' You will have no idea what a shared consciousness is or whether it even exists, but the observation about the flock, firmly stated as a fact, carries a profound aura of truth. Others may dispute these words, but the observation has a depth beyond simple fact. It opens up conceptual possibilities far beyond the here and now.

Other examples of insightful observations might be:

- It's funny how kids always behave so well when their parents aren't around.

- Sport is always so much more gripping if you have a background story to the event.

These observations are not simple factual accounts of events. They are intriguing generalisations embedded in a casual remark. They say much about life as viewed from the other's perspective, and they invite the listener to extrapolate out from the observation and gain new insights into their own experience of the world.

Wise observations are often simple gifts and benefits that we receive from others who come from a different perspective. For example, if we pick up hitchhikers when travelling, we often find that their world view is very different from our own.

An apparently vacuous conversation will usually ensue about seemingly random topics. But somewhere along the way an interesting observation or comment about life will occur. The interest usually occurs because of a point of difference. It might be made from a teenage perspective to the middle-aged, or by a destitute vagrant to a well-heeled businessman. Invariably, after dropping off a grateful hitchhiker, the driver will be left with plenty to ponder about the vagaries of life and its many splendoured shades. And the same opportunity for thoughtful reflection and insight also arises for the hitchhiker.

To be a detached observer of life is to be wise. To comment dispassionately on what is happening around you, without judgment or rancour but with an air of personal conviction, is to be wise. In this mode we are simply reflecting in public about the general patterns that we see. We are holding up a mirror to the world, and we are gently inviting others to share in our perspective.

'Life can be cruel', 'life has many twists and turns', 'life giveth, and it taketh away', 'there is never a dull day …' are all examples of very broad comments that capture general themes to specific events.

Next time you watch the news on TV, try making a wistful, non-judgmental comment at the end of each item. It won't be long before you are sighing wisely, 'Ahhh … that's politics for you' or 'Is there no end to the lack of respect in the world these days?' You are holding back from the urge to express a strongly held opinion about each and every indignant story that is served up. Instead, you are simply reflecting 'wisely' on the way the world seems to be unfolding, and you are calmly extracting a broader perspective on current affairs.

Insights from the street

We often hear of characters who are street-wise, implying that despite lacking formal qualifications, they have learned about life through experience. They might talk about having trained at the *university of life*.

Street wisdom is a fascinating concept as it taps into the very heart of our conceptualisation of wisdom as personal insight gained simply through experience. We do not have to have lived life on the edge to become street-wise. We have all developed great insights about how the world works as the years have passed by. To varying degrees, we inevitably pick up simple concepts and ideas that are worth sharing with others.

Street wisdom: a tale of alcohol and wood

Many years ago I was administering a formal intelligence test to a young offender. He'd failed badly at school, had broken the law and was now applying his cleverness in a range of anti-social ways. He was clearly a quick-minded individual, but his life circumstances to date had not led him down a very positive path. However, everyone enjoyed his quick humour and cheeky quips around the unit where I worked.

One of the questions on the IQ test was, 'In what way are alcohol and wood the same?'

The correct answer required the respondent to reference the fact that both alcohol and wood contain carbon, a fact that my client would never have known. However, he thought hard for a moment before replying earnestly, 'Well, alcohol and wood can both knock you out!'

To my mind it was a brilliant, insightful answer, far more conceptually wise than simply regurgitating some fact from the chemistry syllabus. He'd made an abstract connection that made absolute sense to him.

The scoring protocols for the test did not allow me to credit him with a 'correct' answer. To me this seemed nonsense. My client had found and articulated his own truth — one that resonated more strongly for him than any formal academic truth.

Sadly, we still do not have a psychometric test that adequately assesses street wisdom.

Taxi driver wisdom

Taxi drivers are probably the most celebrated purveyors of street wisdom in the world. They will have an opinion on everything, and they have learned to cut to the chase, being experts in holding brief, succinct conversations.

Next time you are taking a taxi into town from the airport, or back to your hotel, try asking them a second question. For example, you might ask: 'What's the big issue around town at the moment?'

'The local council is spending millions of dollars on a sports complex' or 'There's a plan to build a hotel on conservation land' might be the reply.

'And why do you think that it's so significant for the local people?' could be your second question.

And the answer, whatever it is, will almost certainly involve a wise observation about people and about life.

We can all remember times when a passer-by has dropped a stunning simple truth into a brief conversation with you. You may have been in a waiting room, on a bus or in a queue. It would be a time when you were struck speechless by a comment that made so much sense that you wondered how it could possibly have been uttered by such an ordinary person! This is the essence of street wisdom.

If you seek, you will surely find.

Wise mottos

Mottos are simple phrases that reference core values and have stood the test of time. As such, they have become accepted as general truths about the world. Often, they have been translated from Latin. They carry an inherent sense of wisdom about how to be in the world.

Mottos are often associated with organisations and colleges and declare a founding principle that all graduates are expected to carry forward in their lives. In a similar way, modern organisations will often use strap lines or familiar phrases to promote their brand. The phrase will represent the core values or the purpose of the company, and provide a catchy way of remembering what they are all about.

Examples of mottos for colleges, universities and wise places of learning include:

- Truth conquers all *(Veritas omnia vincit)*.
- Out of darkness comes light *(Ex tenebris venit lux)*.
- Fortune favours the brave (*Audaces fortuna iuvat*).
- Through work, we reach the heights (*Per ardua ad alta*).

113

T-shirts, fridge magnets and car bumper stickers

Even stupid people sometimes take the time to share wise words with others. They may not realise it, but when they choose to display a fridge magnet that says 'All you need is love', they are saying something quite profound.

Likewise, T-shirts, graffitti or bumper stickers proclaiming 'Just do it *NOW*' or 'Make love not war' can be inspirational for others.

My personal motto

If you had a personal motto, what would it be?_____

_____

_____

_____

How can you reference it more frequently in your life?_____

_____

_____

_____

_____

_____

Spiritual insights

All religions provide a rich source of wisdom with regard to living life well. Regardless of whether we are Christian, Buddhist, Muslim, Hindu or atheist, we can often relate to the fundamental creed expressed as a concise formulation of how life should be. Every religion has its founder/leaders and they are universally accepted for their wisdom. They invariably offer their key insights as simple inspirational phrases. For example:

- Jesus: *Seek and you shall find.*
- Buddha: *It is better to travel well than to arrive.*
- Mohammed: *The ink of the scholar is more sacred than the blood of the martyr.*
- Krishna: *Be compassionate and gentle. Show goodwill to all.*

In addition to prescribing moral codes for living a worthy life, religions will also help us to capture themes that we might otherwise struggle to express for ourselves. The prophets can provide a rich source of wisdom, but seem to have fallen out of favour in recent times. However, church services, spiritual gatherings and religious texts still offer a great opportunity to hear their succinct wisdom. It is no accident that we still refer to an 'aha' moment as an *epiphany*, referencing Paul's blinding moment on the road to Damascus many years ago.

Often, it is only when we are at our most needy that we look for these simple spiritual truths. Religious 'aha' experiences can be profound and often set individuals on a lifelong path of self-discovery. Spiritual followers are asking big-picture second questions about life, the universe and everything, and are seeking wise answers in the words of the prophets.

It is extraordinary, and just a little sad, to think about how marginalised spiritual questioning has become. In the modern world of consumerism and televised sport, we seem to have been reduced to a life of factual information and cheap sensory pleasure. The 'why' questions and the 'what's it all about' questions all get left in the too-hard basket.

These days we are not encouraged to think about the bigger picture or to debate some of the bigger moral and philosophical questions that have confronted us for many generations. Sundays are no longer set aside as days of rest and quiet reflection.

Here is your chance to stop and consider whether there is a place in your life for a greater spiritual awareness. If so, then how would it look? What key insights can we gain from different religions and what feels right for us?

One place where spirituality intersects nicely with the secular world is in the quoting of phrases with an apparent religious source. The *Serenity Prayer*, much loved by Alcoholics Anonymous and all related groups that challenge addictions, asks:

> *God, grant me the serenity to accept the things I cannot change,*
> *The courage to change the things I can,*
> *And wisdom to know the difference ...*

It is a widely accepted prayer that applies to a huge number of difficult situations in life. It was written by an American theologian, Reinhold Niebuhr, in 1943 and is actually a contraction of the first verse of a far lengthier prayer. Its real strength lies in its concise summation of a simple truth about how to live life well.

The challenge these days is to re-discover a template for life that provides a guide for living; a personal moral code to live by and a set of simple ideas that anchor our experience. Formal religions used to provide us all with just such a code, but these days, religious wisdom seems to be slipping further and further from the centre stage. Quasi spiritual leaders such as Eckhart Tolle or Deepak Chopra have sprung up among us with wise philosophical perspectives, but often they are simply reworking and reframing established ideas. There are simple truths about the big spiritual picture that transcend any particular code. These days we can pick and we can choose.

The Ten Commandments

For hundreds of years, the Jewish/Christian faith has promulgated the Ten Commandments as the ten simple rules for life. They were usually learned verbatim, and burned into the conscience of believers as absolute truths. They were originally written in stone. And most of us today would still agree that fundamentally, we should all adhere to these Christian values. The Commandments are listed below:

1. Thou shalt have no other gods.
2. Make no graven images or likenesses.
3. Thou shalt not take the Lord's name in vain.
4. Remember the Sabbath day.
5. Honour thy father and thy mother.
6. Thou shalt not kill.
7. Thou shalt not commit adultery.
8. Thou shalt not steal.
9. Thou shalt not bear false witness.
10. Thou shalt not covet thy neighbour's possessions.

Many of the commandments are written in a negative form, prescribing what we should *not* do. Each references an underlying moral weakness to be addressed. If stated positively, however, they become statements that prescribe fundamental human values.

The traditional appraisal of the commandments as a simple list of instructions or rules about life can easily be developed further and brought to life by asking more challenging second questions. For example:

- If you were to review the list above, what is the most personally significant commandment for you? _____

    _____

    _____

    _____

    _____

- If you could translate the words of your significant commandment into a 'simple truth' to guide you in modern life, what would it say? _____

    _____

    _____

    _____

    _____

- What is the paramount commandment? And why? _____

    _____

    _____

    _____

    _____

- Which commandment resonates least with you? What is the underlying principle? What can it teach you about lifting your game? _____

_____

_____

_____

Parables

Many simple spiritual messages are conveyed by short stories or anecdotes known as parables. Parables offer instructive lessons that illustrate a universal principle or truth. Parables are about moral dilemmas and how they are solved. In the Christian tradition, they are stories that Jesus told to help others understand his messages about life. Underpinning each parable is a simple truth, which often comes as a profound 'aha' moment for those who hear them told. Parables, like children's stories, are great vehicles for sharing wise, enduring messages.

Each parable has a simple message to send, and if we ask the right questions about their subtext, we will usually be rewarded with personal insights.

_____

Think about your favourite parable or find one that appeals to you and how you live your life. Write it down and think about the message that it conveys.

My favourite parable is:_____

_____

_____

What lesson does it teach us about life?_____

_____

_____

_____

_____

Summary

In this chapter we have reviewed many sources of wisdom that we have acquired about the world over the years. We have looked at how personal aphorisms, mottos, casual observations, street wisdom, and spiritual guides can all build a reservoir of personal wisdom for us. We learn to see broad patterns and themes that occur in life — themes that we can expect to roll out in our personal lives and in the lives of those around us.

There is much to be gained by simply looking within ourselves and becoming more aware of our personal wisdom. In many ways, this reservoir of experience is the basic platform that allows us to operate confidently in the complex world that we inhabit.

We owe it to ourselves to become as knowledgeable as we can in the ways of the world, and to develop a more astute and discerning understanding of human affairs. We need to challenge ourselves to become smarter — and to become more worldly wise.

Chapter Eight

BEING WISE ABOUT RELATIONSHIPS

When we think about the world we tend to think about the physical world around us, and the common observations that we can all share about life. *Wisdom about the world* is something that is out there and can be objectively discussed with others. Conversely, *wisdom about ourselves* (more of this in the next chapter) is inside us, and is private and unique to us.

However, there is a bridge between the outside world and our private world. This bridge is the link between people and, for many of us, there is a simple truth/belief about life that states: 'The quality of a person's life is largely dependent on the quality of their relationships'.

Our relationship with others is a key factor that determines how fulfilling our life will be. Without a stable family background and an affirming network of friends, life can become very difficult. Becoming wiser about managing relationships is clearly a significant part of everyone's life journey.

There is a wealth of popular wisdom about relationships and what key factors drive fulfilment in this aspect of life. Marriage counsellors, celebrants and ministers will often suggest simple guidelines to couples for a happy life together. Examples of simple maxims about how to relate well to others include:

- Never let the sun go down on an argument.
- Live every day as if it's your last.
- Never lose your sense of humour.
- Make every day a fun day.
- Above all else, be kind to each other.
- Celebrate and respect your differences.

Whether you are married or not, or have been in long-term relationships or not, you will have your own ideas about what a healthy relationship will look like and what the key qualities of a fulfilling relationship would be.

When people are asked, 'What is the most important thing in life?' the most common answer is 'Family'. If we then ask, 'Why is family important?', several factors become immediately apparent. The majority of our social needs are met by family members and it is here that we usually feel secure and nurtured. Family becomes the safe haven for us to return to if we need to. It is also where our values have been shaped and where our basic physical needs have been met.

In our families of origin, we learn our basic wisdom about interacting with others. It is no wonder that a stable family background becomes the basic platform for a fulfilling life.

Conversely, mistrusting, abusive, neglectful or critical relationships in childhood will all contribute to a wide range of presenting problems later on. Being wise about managing relationships is an important life skill, and the topic deserves time for thoughtful reflection.

James meets his stepmother on the road to Damascus

James's mother died when he was fifteen. His father subsequently re-married and a stepmother came into James's life. He was an idealistic young man who found himself embroiled in a series of clashes around everything from washing up to politics. He found it difficult to tolerate her.

Some three years later, on a personal development retreat, he shared his frustrations with the wider group. Among all of the suggestions and advice, one participant's comments stood out.

She simply said, 'In families, everyone only tries to do what they think is for the best.'

For James, in the heightened atmosphere of a retreat, these words struck home. He reports a blinding 'aha' moment, following which he returned home and made a peace with his stepmother that has lasted nearly 40 years.

He still feels an emotional reaction when describing this revelation. Something profound had shifted in his world view. A *simple truth* had fallen into place that lifted him above the battles of the day. In a moment, he had become wiser about managing family relationships.

Relationships provide the best opportunities to actively live out our lives according to our stated values. Interestingly, most of the common values carry an implicit reference to other people. Values such as *respect*, *honesty* and *kindness* all require another person to be the recipient of our beneficence, and they provide the essential platform for relating well. We need to be clear about what we offer and what we expect to receive when relating to other people.

My key values in relating well to others

In order of priority, list below the three essential values that you expect to find in a relationship. Values that you offer to others and values that you would hope to see in their behaviour towards you:

1. _____

2. _____

3. _____

Now close your eyes and think of someone to whom you are close. Imagine that you are simply sitting quietly, facing each other. Breathe deeply and imagine that with each breath, you are radiating your values towards them. Broadcast those values with sincerity. Hold on to that image until you feel truly connected, and then open your eyes. Notice the increased feeling of integrity and vitality to the relationship. You are accessing the basic platform of values which you ideally wish to carry into every interpersonal situation that you come across.

When we interact according to a set of healthy personal values, we engage effectively with others. But if we bully and threaten, or act irresponsibly and impulsively, then we are out of balance with healthy values. Bullies may achieve their objectives in the short term, but lose engagement in the longer term. Conversely, invitations to irresponsibility may initially seem like fun and get engagement in the short term, but there is no sense of purpose or meaning to the relationship in the longer term.

A wise person should interact respectfully and honestly, assuming a basic equality of opinion between two people. They should respect difference. The sense of curiosity and empathy that is inherent to the Socratic questioning style (see Chapter Two) should be reflected in this approach.

Giving advice, feeling sorry, judging or challenging the contributions of others is not the behavioural style of a wise person. The underlying values may be well-intentioned, but these tactics do not support effective personal growth for the other person in the longer term.

Commitment to a shared vision

A cornerstone to any relationship is the concept of *commitment*. A lack of commitment to one's partner will always be a concern, while conversely, the burden of commitment can feel overwhelming.

Commitment is often defined retrospectively as a *promise* made years earlier, perhaps in a church. As time passes, it can feel increasingly like a constraint or a limitation on future options.

Alternatively, if commitment is defined in terms of a *commitment to a shared future vision*, it becomes a relationship enhancer. It feels lighter, provides inspiration and brings energy to the relationship. They are bound not by a contract that they have signed but by a shared future dream.

For couples, sharing a common sense of purpose is the glue that binds them together. Shared ambition is a vitally important aspect of any sustainable relationship. It gives the partnership meaning.

It is rare for a couple to stop and deliberate upon their common purpose in life. They are usually so busy getting on with the practicalities of daily chores that they can only cite job promotions, bigger houses, and financial security as their common goals. But these goals in themselves are not sufficiently fulfilling to justify a lifetime of commitment to one another.

Couples need to reflect more deeply about what they are about as a couple. They need to ask themselves where they are going, and why. They need to ask a shared second question of themselves.

Our shared vision

This exercise is a good one to share with your partner or a significant person in your life. Take some time together to answer the following questions.

- What attracted us to each other? _____

  _____

  _____

- What do we hope to achieve together? _____

  _____

  _____

- Where do we see ourselves in ten years' time? _____

  _____

  _____

- In a sentence, what is our shared vision? _____

  _____

  _____

Answering these questions will quickly identify a sense of purpose and meaning to your relationship. If you struggled to answer, then there is clearly more work to be done and more thoughtful questions to be asked!

Effective communication

A key component to any relationship is communication. The ability to communicate well is a fundamental skill in relating to others, and we tend to learn it by modelling ourselves on the style of those around us. Knowing what information to share, how to share it and when to share it, are all subtle but essential judgments that we are continually required to make.

There is great wisdom required to get your message across effectively. We need to be clear, succinct and structured. We need to pitch our message in terms that the listener understands. We need to listen to their responses. We need to set an appropriate emotional tone and keep focused on the desired outcome.

It has been said that the golden rule of communicating well is to communicate to others as you wish to be communicated to. However, the platinum rule of communication is to communicate with others *as they wish* to be communicated with. Some like their messages straight and to the point. Others like a softer approach. Some like the personal touch, while others like to discuss things as a group. Some like to talk, while others prefer a written summary.

In personal relationships we are usually communicating one on one, verbally, and we don't generally beat around the bush.

Discovering your communication style

To clarify your personal wisdom about communication styles, consider your answers to the following questions.

- What, in your opinion, is the key component to effective communication? _____

  _____

  _____

- What is your favourite saying about communicating well? _____

  _____

  _____

- What are your personal strengths in communicating? _____

  _____

  _____

- What areas might need some work? _____

  _____

  _____

Wise individuals communicate calmly and succinctly. They offer their contributions with respect and for the benefit of the listener. They do not grandstand or force their opinions on others. They simply float ideas and possibilities, letting the words speak for themselves.

Wise words are not up for debate. They are delivered as a gift, to be accepted thoughtfully or respectfully set aside. An individual's truth may not necessarily be a universal truth, but they are sharing an idea that works for them and probably has value for others to consider as well.

Resolving conflict

Conflict between people is a common reason for seeking guidance from a wise person. Differences of opinion can erupt suddenly and unpredictably in any relationship. Because we are seeing the situation from our own particular point of view, we are not necessarily in the best place to take a dispassionate overview. Around conflict, the accepted guideline is always to pull up from the specifics, and to consider the bigger picture. To pull back and find a higher level of agreement that becomes the platform for discussion.

In legal proceedings around relationship break-ups and separation, a judge might well ask a series of second questions that invite a combative couple to pause and reflect upon what common ground they have. So often in conflict, the focus is on the points of difference, and the wider points of agreement are ignored. In addition, we tend to *polarise* opinions in a heated debate by reacting to each other's point of view.

The more a partner wants to spend money, the more the other will try to save. The tougher a parent would like to be, the softer the other becomes. They are often simply trying to bring a sense of balance to the situation.

The key role of a mediator is to ask questions that re-focus the discussion on future-oriented possibilities, rather than indulge in a retrospective discussion of fault and blame. Focusing on the creation of a future plan is always the best way out of a dispute.

Judges are well-respected as the 'wise owls' that they are. Although guided by case law, often they are called upon to exercise their discretion in resolving a conflict. In many cases, they are making decisions on the basis of what they have experienced both professionally and personally. Their wisdom is simply the wisdom of their experience, but their questions will largely focus on the way ahead.

Resolving a simple dispute

Think of a small example of current conflict in your life. Summarise it briefly here.

_____

_____

_____

Now consider the following second questions:

- What values do you have in common with the other person? ____

_____

_____

- What points of agreement do you share? _____

_____

_____

- What would a suitable compromise look like to someone looking in? _____

_____

_____

- How can you both move forward with a sense of dignity and self-respect? _____

_____

_____

Conflicts occur all the time in our lives. They are an inevitable part of the journey. We have to deal assertively with them to make sure that they stay as molehills, not mountains, in our lives.

_____

Problems invite us to focus in on the situation and to become overly analytical. However, the converse skill of pulling back and reflecting on the bigger picture is crucial. How many times have we been stuck searching for a solution to a problem, only to see the answer when we give up and stop? It's at times like these that 'aha' moments occur. The quality of our lives will lift up appreciably as we see the bigger picture.

Making time to have fun

Every healthy relationship requires us to enjoy being with each other. Whether we are talking about work teams, sports teams or personal relationships, we need to be able to relax and laugh together. The chemistry and connection that comes from shared humour and appreciation of life's pleasures is crucial.

It's about just *being* together rather than *doing* things together. The honeymoon period in any relationship involves fun and indulgent pleasure. Fooling around is a much under-valued activity in this achievement-oriented age. We expect ourselves to be purposeful and goal-oriented all the time, and chatting aimlessly about family matters or the local news of the day is generally frowned upon. Time is money and we don't allow ourselves to let it slip through our fingers.

However, walks on the beach, leisurely lie-ins, and meaningless phone calls all have their place. The sense of connection between people generally occurs at exactly those times defined by a *lack* of purpose. When we stop together to reflect on life, we are celebrating our shared experience and we feel closer for it.

Imagine being on a cycle tour with a friend. You pedal fast for several hours through the most amazing countryside. You are exhilarated and breathless. It's a great ride. However, it's only when you stop for lunch or to admire the view, that you can appreciate the shared moment. Your momentum is lost, but the sense of connection has increased. You are *being*, not *doing*.

Are you connecting in your relationships?

- Do you have a healthy balance of *being* and *doing* in your relationship? _____

  _____

  _____

- Do you make time for shared reflection? _____

  _____

  _____

- What are your best points of agreement? _____

  _____

  _____

- What are your biggest challenges? _____

_____

_____

_____

Good relationships always make time for sharing quality time together. Whether we are sharing the quieter sanctuaries in life or the more exuberant playgrounds, we find a deeper connect by letting go of our drive to achieve, focusing instead on enjoying the here and now with each other.

What is love?

Love is an abstract concept. You cannot see, touch or hear love. By its nature, love can only be understood by asking ourselves second questions. It is a dull and tragic life where definitions of love are not sought out and shared. It is what holds us all together.

We can be blinded by love, and we can be guided by love. We hope that 'love springs eternal' and sometimes, when we look around, we can 'feel the love'. Popular songs will tell us that 'love is in the air', or that 'all you need is love'.

Many inspirational quotes and homilies make reference to love. We are often given advice on how to find love and how to cherish it. We are encouraged to embrace the experience and we look for wise counsel when love is lost. Many, many inspirational quotes offer sage advice about love. But there is a universal question that we all face at some stage in our life: 'What is love?'

Coming from a position of love in relation to the world, and in our attitude to others who occupy the same space, is a laudable ambition. If we carry a generosity of spirit towards others, then we will also feel good in ourselves.

The love of family and friends surrounds us like a warm cloak. We should savour the concept and nurture its place in our lives.

When we are in love it feels as if we are truly connected as one with the other. We are aflame with positive feelings. It is a great place to be.

Similarly, being loved is a wonderful experience. Feeling the warmth of another's affection is a very comforting emotion. Parents, family and friends can all step in to provide this fundamental sense of being nurtured emotionally.

Conversely, if we don't feel loved, we keenly feel its absence in our lives.

When we reflect on times that we have been in love, we can start to come up with answers for ourselves in understanding love. Try the following exercise.

The meaning of love

Think back to a time when you were head over heels in love. Remember how it felt. It may have been a teenage romance; it may have been a childhood toy or teddy bear; or it may have been felt at the birth of your son or daughter. Ask yourself some second questions about love because being clear about your personal definition of love is a great step towards a deeper appreciation of life. Wise individuals understand the meaning of love.

- How did you feel? _____

_____

_____

- What did you notice about yourself/the world around you? ___

  _____

  _____

  _____

- In what way were your thoughts different from usual? _____

  _____

  _____

  _____

- What does love mean for you? _____

  _____

  _____

Being clear about your personal definition of love is a great step towards a deeper appreciation of life. Wise individuals understand the meaning of love.

When we are in love with life, we are truly living at the top of our game. Radiating a loving, beneficent attitude will usually be returned in kind. And when we can learn to love ourselves, then we are truly experiencing what life is all about.

'Without love, there is nothing' — this simple truth emphasises the universally accepted importance of love. When we lose a loved one, our grief is an aching reminder of the importance of love. Without love, life feels empty, lonely and hollow.

Your personal secrets to a happy relationship

Every day we read in the paper about a couple celebrating 50 or 60 years of marriage. There is usually a cosy photograph of them cuddling and smiling, accompanied by the story of how they met (usually at a dance) and the historical details of their life together.

But then always, absolutely always, the reporter will hit them with a second question: 'What is your secret to a happy marriage?'

The answers are often formulaic and reasonably predictable. Values such as *forgiveness, tolerance* and *honesty* always feature strongly. A *sense of humour* also seems mandatory. We will also often hear the simple maxim: '*Never let the sun go down on an argument*'.

Although trite, the following simple exercise can give us considerable food for thought. If you were to be asked about your own secret to a happy relationship, what would you say? What is your personal wisdom, acquired over the years, about relating well to others?

_____

My key insights about relating well to others

Of all the things that I've heard or read about relationships, the following three simple truths are the most significant:

1. _____

_____

2. _____

_____

3. _____

_____

These are my personal secrets to a happy relationship, and they are secrets that I am happy to share.

Summary

In this chapter, we have looked at our personal wisdom regarding relationships. We have considered the usefulness of seeking clearer personal definitions of some abstract concepts such as *commitment* and *love*, and we have also looked at what *values* seem most important to us in maintaining a healthy relationship. We have noted the need for partnerships to have a sense of common purpose and a clearly articulated shared vision.

We have also looked at three key relationship issues concerning a) effective *communication*, b) the resolution of *conflict*, and c) the importance of spending *quality time* together. Each of these reviews provides opportunities to learn something new about ourselves — to gain deeper insight into how we relate to others.

We have briefly strayed into the wonderful world of trying to define *love*, but righted the ship by finally asking ourselves the biggest and most formulaic question of all: *What is our personal secret for a happy relationship?*

The answer is obviously not really a *secret* as such. It's just a simple truth. And invariably it *is* simple. And invariably it *is* true.

Chapter Nine

BEING WISE ABOUT YOURSELF

Knowing oneself and one's personal values is the cornerstone of self-confidence and self-esteem. There is an inherent stability and authority about someone who knows who they are. They carry themselves with an air of calm self-assurance.

Being able to walk through life on a platform of wisdom is an empowering experience. In order to do this, we need to have asked a series of second questions of ourselves. We need to be able to answer several variations of Dr Foster's Good Question. Instead of thinking about other people, or perhaps the world in general, this time we need to focus on ourselves. We need to ask ourselves, 'Having lived life thus far, what have I learned about myself?'

We shall be looking at our self-image and will be considering how to construct a positive view of ourselves that celebrates our strengths and personal characteristics. We shall be affirming our self-knowledge and our self-esteem.

Essentially, we shall be addressing one of life's most fundamental questions ... the question that asks: *Who am I?*

The exercises in this chapter cannot be completed quickly and initially may seem too daunting or too overwhelmingly vast to answer. You will be invited to review a wide range of factors that have influenced your life and to consider how they have shaped your personal identity.

You can dwell deeply on each question, looking for a perfect reply, or you can jump in with the first answer that occurs to you. Wisdom can be found using either kind of response style — the deliberate or the spontaneous. The main thing is to distil the key messages and learnings that you have received in your life so far and generate a summary of the most significant personal truths that resonate with you.

When these truths are brought together, you will develop a far more structured sense of the person you feel you really are.

Our identity and self-image is shaped by many factors. Following are separate influences that help to determine our sense of self.

Messages from your father (or father figure)

Take a few minutes to remember situations that you have shared with your father in the past. Clear your mind and allow images to surface of times when you have been together. Remember some special moments that you shared.

Even though he may not have said much, what was it about you that he enjoyed? What did he value in you that made him proud? Imagine what he might say if asked to describe the best aspects of your personality. Write your answer in the space opposite.

Your father's quotes:

• The thing that I like most about you is: _____

_____

_____

_____

_____

• Of all the things that I've told you about living life well, the most important thing to remember is: _____

_____

_____

_____

_____

Messages from your mother (or mother figure)

Now repeat the exercise for your mother. Settle back and take the time to remember times when you were together. As an infant, a child, a teenager and beyond. Remember the conversations that you've had, and remember what aspects of your personality she valued and that made her proud.

Also, try to extract the key message that your mother would wish to give you about living life well. Perhaps imagine her final farewell to you, where she has one last chance to emphasise her advice. Complete the following sentences.

Your mother's quotes:

• The thing that I like most about you is: _____

_____

_____

_____

_____

- More than anything, don't ever forget that the most important thing in life is to: _____

_____

_____

_____

Messages from your family

Look back and remember the key values that were inherent in your family of origin. For some families, the emphasis is on *mutual support* and *kindness*. For others, the key drivers might be *competition* and *success*.

Fun, service to others, self-reliance, curiosity. What were the defining characteristics that were encouraged by your family when you were a child? Complete the following sentences.

- My family encouraged me to be: _____

_____

_____

- We were all taught to be: _____

_____

_____

• If our family had a motto, it would be: _____

_____

_____

Reflecting on your social identity

If you widen the analysis to think more broadly than just your family influences, you will be aware that there is also a social and cultural context to your identity. Your family of origin occupied a certain place in society and, as such, carried certain values. You may now find yourself living out those values or perhaps shifting to a social role that suits you better.

Families where the main income is drawn from a business will probably be promoting social ideals such as *ambition* and *achievement*. These are the stories that are shared during family meals. But if the breadwinners are professionals, such as lawyers or doctors, then they will be probably be promoting academic *excellence* and *ethical standards*. And for those working in the social services or government sector, then the emphasis might be on social *fairness* and *equality*.

For individuals in straightforward employment at an hourly rate, their values will probably revolve around the importance of *reliability* and solid *dependability*. Alternatively, for those who depend on welfare support, the added sense of desperation might focus the key lifestyle message on *acceptance* of life's twists and turns, and learning to make the most of any opportunities that arise.

As we swim through the different social currents in society, we tend to adopt the world view of our own particular stream. It is important not to stereotype the beliefs of each sector, but nonetheless we cannot help but be influenced by the differing prevailing attitudes and beliefs of our particular social network.

Consider the following questions:

- What is the most obvious simple truth about life that is shared by your social network? What do you collectively value? _____

_____

_____

_____

- What personal variations might you decide to make to this general truth? _____

_____

_____

_____

One of the more interesting aspects of reflection is to realise that different political beliefs, social perspectives and community opinions are all simply collective assumptions. They seem so true when we talk, but they are simply a lens through which we all choose to see the world. It is this diversity of assumed truths that makes election time so interesting in a democratic society.

The influence of your national identity

If we widen out the analysis of our inherent lifestyle values beyond social influence, we can consider *national identity*. Every nation has a stereotypic image or characteristic that espouses certain values. For example, there are some countries where the people are considered to be hard-working and others where the people are more relaxed. Some nationalities are seen as doggedly persistent, while others tend to be more flexible in nature. There are countries well-known for punctuality and timekeeping, and others for whom time doesn't really seem to matter.

Every nation has its general characteristics, and its people often carry them too.

Take some time to reflect on your national identity. Consider the personal qualities that it promotes, and whether or not you are personally aligned with them.

- Write down your nationality: _____
- What are the three key attributes that are commonly referenced about the citizens of your country?

1. _____

2. _____

3. _____

Circle or underline the one that is most important to you.

Understanding your culture

A subtly different concept to nationhood is that of *culture*. Culture, according to the *Collins English Dictionary,* is defined as 'the total of the inherited ideas, beliefs, values, and knowledge which constitute the shared bases for social action'. Culture describes shared traditions, social expression and tastes, and the *mutual enlightenment* that arises from them.

Seeing culture defined in this way (mutual enlightenment) resonates fantastically with the purpose of this book. In connecting with a culture, a series of light-bulb moments will occur, where we see the world and our place in it from a defined perspective. It shapes who we are and how we behave. Culture clearly provides a great source of personal wisdom and insight.

The cultures of indigenous peoples such as NZ Maori, Australian Aborigines or Native Americans are even more clearly defined and are always rich in metaphor. There will be hundreds of simple sayings and phrases, many of which relate back to the land in a very powerful way. As such, the wisdom of indigenous people is anchored in a profound connection with the Earth. If you relate to a particular culture, then your identity will be strongly determined by the stories and lessons that are handed down through the generations.

If you feel closely aligned with an indigenous culture, then answer the following questions.

My indigenous culture

Write down the essential features of your culture that you can identify closely with.

What defines us as a people?	What are the core beliefs that distinguish us from others?	What are our core values?

Cultures are not necessarily race-based. Within society we can also subscribe to specific groups that have cultures of their own. Examples might include a *sporting* culture, an *academic* culture, a *hippie* culture, an *artistic* culture or a *business* culture. Spiritual groups or community interest groups also have their defining cultures. There are a range of different social cultures and it is largely a matter of personal choice as to where you fit in.

Each culture will have its own identifying characteristics, and the members will be drawn to the group because of them. The shared activities, values and aspirations of individuals who share a culture will help shape the personal identities of them all. Common themes and values will be readily apparent.

An example might be that you grow your own vegetables, enjoy health foods, take herbal supplements and shop at local farmers' markets. Your culture could be defined as an 'organic' culture. Your key values are sustainability, health, nature and self-care. A common slogan or simple phrase that captures the ideals might be 'Healthy food, healthy people'.

Alternatively, you might enjoy running and cycling and attend gym classes regularly. You might subscribe to a fitness magazine and carry a water bottle with you wherever you go to re-hydrate. Your culture could be described as one of 'physical fitness' and the key values would be vitality, strength, energy and motivation. Your gym's slogan might be 'No pain, no gain. No limits'. You might find that these simple phrases come readily to mind in response to a wide variety of situations in your life. They have come to represent a generic personal wisdom for you.

My social culture

List the social cultures or interest groups to which you feel aligned. Against each of these, write down the values that characterise the members of that group. Perhaps you could then add a one-sentence summary of what that culture stands for.

My social cultures	The key values/ ideals	A simple phrase that captures the spirit

Knowing the key attributes of your social culture provides a great context for self-awareness and is an important part of knowing yourself.

Significant stories from your life so far

The nature of the stories that we tell about ourselves reveals a great deal about who we are. We may find ourselves expressing themes of success, fun, or surprise. The punchlines to these stories invariably invite others to share in a moment that represents something important to us.

Usually we tell stories for fun and to make others laugh. Personal anecdote functions as light relief or entertainment in social situations. However, in this section of the book, we are looking for more poignant, thought-provoking material — stories that have more depth and relay simple messages about life that are important to you.

Personal anecdotes usually offer key messages about ourselves. They can promote us as humble observers, proud achievers, or fun-loving fools. We need to choose carefully which stories we tell, and the impact that they might have. Our reputations and social identity are often based on them.

Some stories may almost choke us up as we re-tell them. Their impact is so deep and personal that it hurts. The anecdote may have occurred at a very special moment in our life and at a time when we felt in touch with a personal insight worth sharing.

My favourite stories so far

Write down the three most poignant stories from your past that you enjoy sharing with others. They could be dramatic stories, funny stories or simple acts of kindness that you have experienced. Against each story, write down any insights or inherent wise messages that you are sharing.

The favourite stories from my life so far	The story's key message in a nutshell	What it says about me

The favourite stories from my life so far	The story's key message in a nutshell	What it says about me

Learning from adversity

The flip side to reflecting on witty, amusing anecdotes is to reflect more somberly on adversity. Learning from our mistakes, taking the positives out of a disappointing setback and growing in response to adversity, are all common themes around life's journey. 'The wisdom born of pain' is a line that is quoted often.

There will always be events that stand out as major turning points in our lives. It may be the loss of a job, a relationship break-up, an accident, the loss of a loved one or a financial disaster. We will have been thrown out of our comfort zone into a challenging world that we'd have preferred to avoid.

However, often when we look back, we realise that the event actually served to enrich our lives in some way. It added character and we became open to experiencing life in a deeper way.

'If it doesn't kill you, it will make you stronger' is another familiar saying following adversity. When wise individuals look back over their lives, they will invariably identify the low points of their lives as the times when they learned the most about themselves, and learned important lessons about life.

In *A Tale of Two Cities*, Charles Dickens opens with the words: 'It was the best of times, it was the worst of times, it was the age of wisdom …' In this section we are very much concerned with extracting wisdom from 'the worst of times'.

Following bankruptcy, we might hear someone say, 'In the future, I'll always back my intuition rather than follow what others might say' or 'In the future, I will make my major decisions based on reasonable levels of risk, not be driven by the thrill of a gamble'.

Both of these insights are huge 'aha' moments for the individuals concerned. They are significantly different, but both have that key ingredient of resonating with the person concerned as an insightful new truth for them, and will help guide them in the future.

Many poems, songs and inspirational speeches are created in times of adversity. If you look back over the poems and famously wise texts reviewed in Chapter Six, almost all were written in the face of extremely difficult circumstance. From the worst of moments, something special had been learned.

Following a traumatic event, many of us try as hard as we can to stay the same. We try to carry on and not let it affect us. However, these things do affect us, and we can deliberately look for the changes. We can *want* to be changed by circumstance, and to be changed for the better.

Learning from adversity

Write down the worst setbacks or difficulties that you have ever faced — times when you felt overwhelmed, scared and hopeless. Note the emotion beside each event. Then, in one sentence, write down the key learning that you have gained as a result of the experience.

The major setbacks in my life	My emotional reaction	What I learned as a result

Pausing to reflect on the lessons learned in adversity is time well spent. Often we try to push these experiences out of our minds, but there are always lessons to be learned. Experiencing adversity is a key factor that distinguishes the wise from the naive.

Knowing your personal values

The exercises so far have asked you to consider the guiding principles and values that you have acquired in your life. Most of us share a common list of accepted values in our lives. A list that includes values such as *honesty, transparency, respect* and *kindness.*

However, we rarely stop to formally reflect on these values or prioritise them in terms of their importance to us. Values are a key component to self-awareness, and in many ways, they define exactly who we are. Knowing your values means knowing yourself.

We previously noted that the maxim 'be true to yourself' can seem to be a somewhat vacuous phrase. However, it is probably better expressed as an exhortation to 'be true to your values'. If we know our values, then we know how to be true to ourselves.

Values can best be defined as 'the desired qualities of action'. Although they are usually nouns such as 'honesty' or 'integrity', they are not really *things that we have* but instead they simply describe *how we behave.*

There are no right or wrong values and we may prioritise them differently at different times. In different situations, different values may become more important to us.

My five most important values

Write down the five values that are of greatest importance to you.

1. _____

2. _____

3. _____

4. _____

5. _____

Then consider the following questions:

- Which value, in your opinion, is the paramount value?_____

  _____

- Which value most closely describes who you are?_____

  _____

- Which value guides you best in adversity/under stress?_____

  _____

- Which value do you hold uppermost in your relationships with others? _____

  _____

  _____

It is interesting to note that values can serve different functions. One class of values might propel us towards achieving great things in the future (such as excellence, determination or persistence), while another set of values might celebrate our ability to be appreciative and accepting (for example, kindness, respect and humility). Our values very much reflect the way that we wish to live our lives.

Sometimes our values may cause personal conflict. During World War II, harbouring an escaped prisoner whose life is in danger might have required us to prioritise compassion over honesty, where we are obliged to tell lies to keep others safe. Telling a friend that their partner is being deceitful is another example of values in conflict. Should we be honest with our friend or should we keep a confidence that we have been trusted with? It can all become extremely confusing.

The essential message here is that knowing our personal values becomes our road map or compass. It guides our decisions and behaviour. Being familiar with the compass helps us find direction in our lives.

In his popular book *True North: Discover your authentic leadership style*, Bill George uses the concept of a values compass to guide us. This requires us to identify our values to establish 'true north' in our lives, both as business leaders and as individuals. Knowing true north allows us to establish a purposeful and meaningful direction in our life journey.

An authentic leadership style requires us to know ourselves and our values, and to lead in a direction that aligns with them. The personal and the professional merge seamlessly. Our moral compass keeps us on course.

Similar qualities can be found when we think of the purpose of a national flag, especially in the heat of battle. Although a flag does not suggest direction, in a single glance we can connect with all that it represents. There is a strong 'heart' connect with the inherent values that we are fighting for.

Our hearts beat more strongly when we know what we are about. In a moment, we are connecting with our basic values. Anthems and heroic figures have much the same effect. They will usually embody the essence of what we stand for. In a moment, we are instantly connected with our core values.

Are you a follower or a leader, Henry?

During his initial interview at high school, my son Henry met with the school principal and was asked two simple questions:

'Are you a follower or a leader, Henry?' the Principal asked.

'A follower,' he replied. I winced.

'And what qualities do you think make a good follower?'

'Loyalty, reliability and dependability,' Henry replied.

My heart pounded with pride. The second question, so casually asked, had revealed more about my son than I'd ever realised. Henry was wearing his values on his sleeve and we could all see exactly what he stood for.

It was an incisive, wise and skilful question for the Principal to have asked. And Henry's answer left us with a powerful, lasting impression.

There is a great way to access personal values that comes from Acceptance and Commitment Therapy (ACT). This exercise invites you to stop and remember a 'sweet spot' in your life. You are invited to recall a time when you felt totally at one with your ideals, and in tune with your life. To remember a time when you were being totally true to yourself. The therapist will then ask you a series of second questions about the event (my terminology, not ACT's).

1. What does this reveal about what really matters to you?
2. What personal qualities were you showing?
3. How were you treating others/yourself?
4. What does this tell us about how you would like to be in the future?

As people become lost in a sweet memory, whatever it may be, these questions will help them to extract the juice from the fruit. Instead of simply reflecting on happy times gone by, they will find greater clarity about who they are in the present, and how they want to be in the future.

Take a moment to do the exercise below.

Remembering who you really are

Think back to a time when you felt supremely in touch with the world. A moment when you were in tune with life, and were being absolutely true to yourself. Write it down.

_____

_____

_____

_____

Ask yourself the following questions:

- What does it tell me about what really matters in life? _____

_____

_____

- What personal qualities was I showing? _____

_____

_____

- How was I behaving towards others and myself? _____

_____

_____

- What does this tell me about how I would like to be in the future? _____

_____

_____

_____

Finally, extract the inherent core message from your story.

I value: _____

_____

_____

_____

This is who I really am, and who I really want to be: _____

_____

_____

_____

This is how it feels when I am being 'true to myself': _____

_____

_____

_____

_____

For many of us it is hard to define exactly who we are, but if we can identify our core values, then we will be much closer to the answer.

Being true to our personal values means we are living an authentic life. We are aligned with our core principles and, regardless of the circumstances, we know that we are honouring our personal sense of self. We are being *true to ourselves*, and it feels great.

Defining your personal vision — where are you going?

Knowing *who you are* is one thing, knowing *where you are going* is quite another. Unless we have a clear vision of how we would like to be, life will lack purpose or ambition. Having a strong personal vision is a powerful attribute, and one that is easily found by asking good questions.

Most of us have reasonably clear practical goals in our lives. We set financial goals, fitness goals and educational goals. But somehow we rarely seem to convert these goals into a loftier vision for ourselves. We don't really know where we are going in life.

It has been said that 'if you have no goals, then you should make a wish'. If you write the wish down, the goals and the vision will fall naturally from the exercise. We rarely give credit to the role of wishing or dreaming in our lives. In fact, they are often considered to be a waste of time and we are usually discouraged from doing it.

However, cherishing a personal vision is hugely affirming, and it is important that we make space for creative ambition in this way, otherwise we have our eyes cast firmly to the ground as we shuffle pedantically through life. There is no broader sense of purpose or meaning.

A vision is far more than just a set of objectives and goals. To generate a vision we need to ask some lofty questions of ourselves.

- What is my over-arching ideal in life? _____

_____

_____

_____

- What brings me fulfilment? _____

_____

_____

- What issues do I care most deeply about? _____

_____

_____

_____

- If I could choose exactly how my life was to be, how would it look? _____

_____

_____

_____

We saw in Chapter Four how choosing a picture to illustrate *where you would like to be* can quickly help us to access a personal vision. Almost any picture chosen will allow individuals to talk metaphorically, and visually, about how they would like things to be.

A personal vision describes future possibilities or aspirations. Ideally, we have a passionate 'heart' connect with our vision. The vision has to align with our personal values. It should be framed as a positive statement of how you *will* be.

Examples might be:

I will walk calmly through life, accepting the things that I can't change, but assertively grasping the opportunities that come my way. I will radiate confidence, and I will dedicate my life to giving the best of myself in the service of others.

I will offer kindness, humility and compassion at all times. I will respect the opinion of others, but at the same time I will uphold my right to be respected as well. I will live my life mindfully and will stay fully present in the Now.

I will embrace life's opportunities to the full. I will bring energy, dynamism and enthusiasm to any situation that I come across. I will constantly look for any opportunity to learn or have fun, and will have no regrets when I'm gone.

Each of these statements provides a clear description of both a way of being and a way of behaving. They describe the individual's personal values, and are all stated definitively. They are all achievable, laudable and affirming. For each of the individuals concerned, there will be a far stronger sense of purpose to life as they stride forward, knowing what their personal vision is like.

My personal vision

Complete the following sentence, using no more than 50 words. Describe how you will behave and the values that you will promote.

I will _____

_____

_____

_____

_____

_____

_____

Defining your personal vision is possibly the most important exercise in this book. It goes hand in hand with the exercise where we defined our values. It tells you where you want to go. It provides an aspirational goal of how you would like to be. Once you have established your vision, all decisions and choices can be referenced against it. It provides a guiding light. It is the kernel of wisdom about self.

Summary

This chapter provides the central core to our sense of personal wisdom. It asks us to consider who we are and what we stand for. It requires us to look at the key factors that have influenced us and that make us who we are now.

We reviewed messages from our *mothers, fathers* and our *families of origin*. We looked at the *social, cultural* and *national* influences that may have helped shape our identity, and went on to consider the inherent messages that we learned from the *best of times* and the *worst of times* in our past.

Finally, we have looked at our *values* and our *personal vision*, and noted how living consistently with our values is synonymous with *being true to ourselves*.

Knowing oneself is a fundamental attribute of being wise. Reflecting on oneself and asking good questions about who we are is always time well spent. The more that we discover about ourselves, the richer our life will be. We cannot hope to understand life properly if we have not learned to understand ourselves first.

Chapter Ten

LEARNING FROM YOUR INTERESTS AND YOUR PAST EXPERIENCES

This chapter falls into two distinct parts. The first part looks at our leisure interests and hobbies; the specific knowledge and experience that we accumulate as we relax and play offers many insights that are more broadly applicable to life in general. If we stop to reflect on what we have learned, we can often find simple gems that are worth savouring and perhaps sharing with others.

The second part reviews our personal life history, considering what lessons we can learn from specific parts of our unique journey. At each stage of our life we gain insights that we could later share with others. Embedded within any past experience, we can usually find a thought-provoking message about living life well.

Learning from your specific leisure interests

It is a huge mistake for us to think that leisure interests are simply something that we do to fill in the emptier parts of our day. Increasingly, our leisure time is the *only* time that we have to pursue activities that are truly important to us. It is discretionary time. It is time when we can truly relax into being ourselves. The activities that we choose might seem to be a little arbitrary, but invariably, the inherent qualities of the interest will strongly reflect our own character.

If we love orderliness and structure, we may collect things. If we love competition, we will compete. If we love to relax, we will find an interest that encourages this. Whatever our interests, we will quickly adopt the generally accepted principles that underscore the activity.

We may say that 'The first rule of entertaining guests is to get the music right' or, 'When cooking, timing is everything'. These are expressed *opinions* masquerading as *facts*. They are usually based on personal experience and they tend to promote the idea that we can learn from simple rules.

Over our lifetime we develop a range of interests and the guiding principles are commonly agreed to by all who share the pastime. As time passes, our wisdom accumulates. We become useful people to turn to for advice around the specific topic.

Whether we are gardeners, stamp collectors, pigeon fanciers or musicians, we will develop an array of familiar wise sayings. These are often specific to the interest, but they are also more generally applicable to life in a far broader sense.

Any specific interest can provide an enlightening perspective on life that often adds colour to a debate. If we are talking about leadership, for example, we can draw on the wisdom of how conductors lead orchestras, how sheep dogs lead sheep, how politicians lead their parties, or how queen bees make decisions.

Each specific interest will have something to contribute to the discussion and it is the diversity that usually creates the opportunity for insight.

There are several very popular recreational interests that naturally lend themselves to providing wise words about living life well. Gardening, cooking and sailing are three particular examples, and we shall look at each in turn.

Gardening

Gardening provides a rich, generic source of wisdom. Most of us have at least a passing interest in growing things, and carry varying degrees of wisdom about the process. Many gardeners are a veritable mine of factual information, but they can easily remain stuck at this level of simple information exchange.

Experts can tell you how to take cuttings, when to plant and where to plant. More annoyingly, they can often also tell you a plant's Latin name under the Linnaeic classification. At this level of gardening, your only hope is to read as much as you can and try to remember it all.

However, gardening also represents a great theatre for extracting broader lessons about life. Gardening themes have a wonderful application to life beyond the garden wall.

Gardeners have a great connection with nature. They share a great deal of wisdom that has been handed down through the generations. The basic principles of growing plants have remained unchanged over many centuries. A wealth of phrases and catchy sayings has evolved that capture the essence of good practice.

Examples include:

- Plant on the shortest day of the year, harvest on the longest. (For garlic only!)

- A wise gardener anticipates June in January.
- Without good composting, a garden is nothing. Composting completes the cycle of life.
- The tallest trees have the deepest roots. (Not necessarily true!)
- Even more loftily, Gandhi suggested that 'to forget how to dig the earth and to tend the soil is to forget ourselves'.

To garden well is to live life well. When we garden, we are obliged to work with Nature, and to strike a balance between beauty and productivity. A well-proportioned garden, laid out carefully with a considered, over-arching plan, will provide a deeply fulfilling addition to our broader lives.

A garden teaches us a lot about living life well. It also teaches us a lot about ourselves.

Even if you don't have a garden, you could ask yourself the following second questions:

- If I were to grow a plant from seed, what type of plant would it be? _____

  _____

- If I had a garden, what could I learn about living life well? _____

  _____

  _____

And for those of you who do have a garden:

- What is the golden rule of gardening for me? _____

  _____

  _____

- What has been the biggest lesson that I have learned? _____

_____

_____

- What is the most pleasurable time of the year for me? Why? ____

_____

_____

These are the kind of questions that come more naturally to gardeners when they are idly watering the garden or relaxing with a cup of tea on the garden seat. Gardening offers many opportunities for personal reflection about living life with a natural rhythm.

In replying to these more abstract questions, even the most practical of gardeners will be obliged to pause and lift up from the task in hand. Instead of concentrating on how to prune a rose or where to plant a tree, they will be thinking instead about where gardening fits into their lives, and what wisdom they have gained from their favourite leisure pursuit. They can learn to recognise and savour the insights that Mother Nature has taught them.

Cooking

Cooking is another practical activity that evolves into a leisure interest for many of us. We watch cooking programs on television, we buy cookery magazines and we share new recipes with friends. Cooking has a wonderful ability to continually re-invent itself, such that there is always something new to learn.

However, just as we saw in the gardening section, it is a rather limiting perspective to simply exchange recipes and handy hints about technique.

The majority of cooking conversations operate at this level, but each would be significantly enhanced if a 'wise lesson' could be added as a final flourish.

If we think about the personalities and themes of our favourite TV chefs, we invariably find inherent values in their style of cooking that also tell us something about ourselves. Each chef will have their own set of personal catchphrases and sayings that they use as they create a dish. Do they pay meticulous attention to detail and strive for the perfect recipe? Or do they go with the flow and let the dish evolve? Is the emphasis on healthy ingredients or more on indulgent pleasure? Do they create exotic fusions across different cultures or do they specialise in a certain style. And what are the key descriptors of that style?

_____

When you cook, how would you describe your style?

_____

_____

What are your key messages to others about how to cook well?

_____

_____

_____

Cooking isn't just about preparing food. It's a passion and it's an art form. The kitchen is a place where we can learn so much about how we want to be and how we want to live.

Sailing

I personally love sailing, so you will have to forgive me if I indulge a little here! Sailing provides a rich metaphor for life and many of life's tricky moments can be understood with reference to a sailing dilemma.

Sailing with a *following wind*, or into a *headwind*, or sailing on a *broad reach*, all have their psychological equivalents in the wider world. And sailing through *the doldrums*, where all momentum is lost, leads to a miserably depressive state.

Life can be either *plain sailing* or else we are obliged to face the turbulence of a *stormy voyage* through life's upsets.

More than most leisure activities, sailing requires us to *trim our sails to suit the prevailing wind*. When sailing in *stormy waters*, we focus on the strength of our vessel rather than the size of the waves ahead. In general, we all prefer the opportunity to *sail on an even keel*.

Sometimes we find ourselves sailing in *uncharted waters*. But then again, *ships were never built to stay in safe harbours*. Old sea-salts (who also probably *had a girl in every port*) will remember the old adage *any port in a storm* when facing adversity.

We *weigh anchor* and we *set sail* (on *life's rough seas* — a line from my old school hymn). We *drop anchor* and we *heave to*. We also know that *neither time nor tide wait for man*, and we never drink alcohol until the sun drops *over the yard arm*.

Whatever else sailing brings to one's life, a rich ocean of wisdom and metaphor is one undeniable benefit. Sailing enthusiasts bring a vibrancy to their everyday conversation that is rarely matched by others.

The wonderful thing about this wisdom, as for the wisdom of any leisure interest, is that the simple truths that are shared are directly applicable to life in general. We all have our turbulent storms and our rudderless moments. But we can also experience those exhilarating surges of adrenaline when under full sail. We do not need to be sailing enthusiasts ourselves to find value and draw upon the metaphor.

Your personal leisure pursuits

Now it is time to consider your personal leisure pursuits. As we have seen previously, every recreational interest can provide us with insight. In addition to learning the specific competencies and skills, we are also learning to think about life in a certain way. Whether you are collecting stamps, sewing quilts or playing bridge, there will be an array of simple truths that are central to the activity.

For example, when playing bridge, *you can only play the hand you are dealt.* This is clearly a widely applicable truth, and it can sometimes provide profoundly appropriate insight to others by lifting them up from their immediate concerns.

In the box below write down your favourite leisure interest and consider the wisdom that it brings to your life.

_____

Wisdom from my leisure pursuits

My favourite pastime is: _____

_____

My favourite anecdote from this interest is: _____

_____

Some wise sayings that are commonly used: _____

_____

The first rule of my interest is to: _____

_____

The key thing to know about my interest is: _____

_____

_____

The fundamental personal qualities required to succeed are: _____

_____

_____

The most significant thing that it has taught me about myself is: _____

_____

_____

The next time you are with a fellow enthusiast, you might like to casually ask them the same questions. They are all second questions and they may generate surprising replies!

_____

Do not be shy about sharing details of your personal interests. Try to reference your leisure activities in your everyday conversation. You will be sharing personal insights and you will also be strengthening your visibility as a person. Your perceived depth of character by others will increase as a result.

Learning from our unique past experiences

As we travel through life we each follow a unique path. We acquire specific skills and knowledge along the way that give us the opportunity to become wise. We learn to extract general principles from our personal catalogue of experience that helps give meaning and helps us to make sense of the world.

Regardless of how boring our lives may seem, we have all had different experiences that provide personal insights to compare and contrast with others. We can extract gems of wisdom from the most unlikely or tedious of situations. There are always interesting points of difference for others to consider.

If we choose to share our past experiences with others in a thoughtful way, we find that it adds depth and strength to our character. It adds to our social identity and to our public profile.

A story from my past

Sit back and relax. Let your mind wander back to your past. Think of a story that you have often told others from your past. It could be an amazing experience, a funny experience, or a tragic experience. Write down the key details of the story below.

_____

_____

_____

_____

_____

_____

_____

_____

_____

Now deliberately finish the story by lifting the narrative to a higher level. Summarise by completing the following sentence:

And the key thing that I took away from that incident in my life was:

_____

_____

_____

_____

_____

Many of us are reluctant to talk too much about ourselves. We carry a natural inhibition about self-disclosure or we may have learned that it is unwise or boorish to say too much about ourselves. Clearly it is a judgment call as to how much to disclose and when. Sometimes we hear far too much from some people who talk excessively about 'the good old days' of a former life.

However, briefly referencing the key insights from a previous experience can be a useful contribution to a discussion. And asking for the 'summary insight' when others are talking about their own past experiences will also lift the tone and pace of the conversation.

Reflecting quietly on your past and choosing not to share the lessons learned is like keeping playing cards in your hand, close to your chest. They have no value until you lay them down on the table. And we all have some great cards to play.

In reviewing your own past catalogue of thought-provoking experiences, the following exercises will elicit a number of key personal insights that you may never have previously stopped to consider.

Stories from your childhood

The older we get, the more we repeat time-honoured stories that have been frequently told about our childhood. We selectively remember certain stories that amuse us and tell others a little more about who we are. Our parents also have a great deal of influence over our recall of childhood by the anecdotes that they routinely tell.

These are our formative years. We are blank canvasses upon which we are evolving and learning the basics of life. Certain core themes will be emerging for each of us in different ways during this period of our lives.

_____

A favourite anecdote from my childhood
Write down a quick summary of a favourite story or a strong memory from your childhood.

_____

_____

_____

_____

_____

What is the _key learning_ that you take from this story? _____

_____

_____

What would the *take home message* be to others?_____

_____

_____

In a sentence, what does this say about your formative years? _____

_____

_____

Stories from your teenage/student years

As we strike out into life on our own, we take more control of the experiences that we have. As teenagers or as students, we start to explore life for ourselves. We seek out like-minded friends, and we start to find our own way. This is a hugely enlightening period in our lives, where we discover more clearly who we are and what life is all about. We learn about our strengths and our personal qualities, and we also learn from our mistakes. Our teenage and student years are probably the richest source of wisdom through anecdote that we have. The funny stories from this period that we tell against ourselves all carry a strong message about who we are striving to be.

_____

A favourite anecdote from my teenage/student years

Write down a favourite story from your youth — a story that tells us something about the kind of person that you were seeking to become.

- What are the key messages about you as a person now? _____

_____

_____

- What personal qualities did you show? _____

  _____

- How might you have changed since then? _____

  _____

  _____

The chaotic jumble of colourful experiences in our youth allows us to slowly find ourselves. We experiment, we take risks, and we challenge conventional wisdom. The reward for all this is that we define a new wisdom of our own.

In the table below, write down the key incidents that you remember from your transitional years, then identify what these possibly indicated about you then and what insights come out of each story.

Memorable stories from my youth	What this says about me	The key insight to share (in a simple sentence)

Stories from your adult life

As adults, we find ourselves moving through life with a reasonably stable understanding of how the world operates. We know what we believe in, and we feel that we know ourselves just about as well as we can. After the challenges of adolescence, we are now just getting on with things.

However, there is still a great deal to be gained by reflecting on the experiences that we have had. Too often we miss learning opportunities because we were too complacent or made excuses not to learn from potential 'aha' moments.

In adulthood, we have stability, but we also face challenge, opportunities and moments of great satisfaction. We are roaming expansively across life's stage, and in our relative freedom, we can learn so much about who we are and how life can best be lived.

In considering your life as an adult, you can use the table below to list events that made you feel supremely proud, felt like your greatest mistakes, and that represent opportunities missed.

Against each event, write down what the story says about you, and then consider what lessons may be drawn about life in general. Is there anything that you would like to do to change or enhance things for yourself in the future?

Key learning events in my adult life	What this says about me and my values	What the story tells us about life
I felt really proud when...		

Key learning events in my adult life	What this says about me and my values	What the story tells us about life
My greatest mistake was when...		
The biggest lost opportunity occurred when...		

In reviewing our lives in this way we become far more self-aware. By using structured reflection, we can extract the key insights and our learnings about life. A similar thing happens when we read autobiographies. The author tells their story and then invariably shares the wisdom and insights that they have gained from their story so far. We benefit as a result.

You do not have to be famous to be wise. We all have the opportunity to write down the narrative of our lives, and we can all extract and share the key insights from the experiences that we've had. The events do not need to be exotic or dramatic. Indeed, some of the most poignant wisdom comes from simple everyday events.

Years ago, I was sitting in a men's discussion group where we were all sharing stories about the male urge to problem-solve in response to challenging situations. One participant, deep in thought, suddenly piped up, 'You know, yesterday I dropped a bottle of milk as I lifted it out of the fridge. It smashed all over the floor. I suddenly realised that in some situations, you just can't put things back together. You just have to accept it, make the best of things, and move on.'

We were all silenced by his anecdote. He'd said just the right thing at the right time. We all took his wisdom on board, and the associated insight. After an hour or so of opinionated intellectual debate, we had suddenly arrived at a succinct and collectively satisfying conclusion.

Sometimes in life you have to just accept things, make the best of them and move on.

The decades of my life

Some people prefer to systematically review their lives in ten-year chunks. The table below is laid out to invite reflection on these different stages of your life. Try to capture the key themes of each period, and what simple wisdom can be extracted and succinctly shared as a result of those ten-year blocks of life experience.

Your age	Key memories	Key insights
0–10		
11–20		
21–30		

Your age	Key memories	Key insights
31–40		
41–50		
51–60		
60+		

In many ways, these simple exercises traverse the whole purpose of the book. If you systematically trawl back through your memories, you will find wisdom. The key technique, however, lies in paying attention to the right-hand column.

How often do we reflect fondly on past events simply as happy memories without bothering to then ask ourselves what we learned or how the experiences subsequently informed our lives? Even if we are only remembering a dull commute to work on public transport many years ago or a character who irritated us at the time, we can now look back with the wisdom of hindsight and capture lessons to be learned in the bigger picture.

Remembering the Sixties

I once was watching a TV documentary about music in the 1960s, called *All You Need is Love: The story of popular music*. Towards the end of the program, a series of ageing rock stars all agreed that the 1960s was all about love. But suddenly, on came Abbie Hoffman, a human rights activist from the period, who angrily claimed: 'No! The Sixties wasn't about love. It was all about human rights marches. It was about Vietnam. It was about Martin Luther King Jr and it was about freedom from oppression. The Sixties wasn't about love, it was about justice!'

In a single moment Abbie had seriously derailed the collective memories of the fuzzy hippy brigade. Dreams of free love were replaced by memories of social activism.

The enduring wisdom about the 1960s was clearly different for different people. The subjective and very personal nature of simple truths was revealed yet again.

Summary

In this chapter we have reviewed the opportunities that we have to gain personal wisdom from our specific leisure interests and from our specific past experiences.

We firstly looked at our hobbies and interests, and paused to consider what the content teaches us about life in general. We looked at what characteristics draw us to such an activity and also considered what the subject matter reveals about our own desired qualities in life.

We then went on to consider what we can learn from the specific past experiences in our lives. We looked at memories drawn from childhood experiences, our teenage years and the challenges that we have faced in adulthood. At each stage there were lessons to be learned about ourselves and about the world in general.

Every single activity and every single experience provides us with a learning opportunity. And the extent to which we actually do learn is determined solely by the extent to which we reflect upon our experiences and interests — and ask ourselves good second questions.

Chapter Eleven

BEING WISE ABOUT YOUR WORK

The major area in life where wisdom comes into its own is at work. We usually train for several years to learn how to do a job, and then we spend several years refining our technique as we go. Along the way we subtly integrate our formal knowledge and our practical experience into a wonderful blend of technical/professional wisdom.

We can train as either *architects* or *builders* in our own field of work. Neither can survive without the other and both have their value. Sometimes it is important that architects learn from practical hands-on experience. Conversely, it is important that builders learn to pull up from the task in hand and find ways to summarise their knowledge into simple, generic truths.

Qualifications only say so much about an individual's ability. There is a wealth of additional material to be found outside of the classroom that is the real measure of a truly wise practitioner.

This book is clearly saying that wisdom is not just found in clever plans or in clever people. It is also to be found in our basic experiences of the real world. Our wisdom at work tends to focus on both our *competencies* and our *character*.

In the early stages of most careers, we often sit at the side of a supervisory mentor for a year or two, with the implicit assumption that we will learn from their past experience. They will share anecdotes and simple maxims about doing the job well. They will gradually share the *tricks of the trade*. In this way, we are trading in the core aspects of wisdom as defined in this book — the wisdom of experience.

This chapter focuses largely on what we have learned in our careers to date, and what concepts might roll out from there that are more generally applicable to life.

Most of us have trained for a career at some stage. We have spent time learning the techniques and theories behind our craft, and have been taught specific knowledge. We have learned about the evolution of the profession or trade, and we learn the specific skills to carry out the work. Once qualified, we are assumed to have the basic skill set to competently do the job.

In addition to our formal training another process is occurring. As we become more experienced in the role, we become wiser about the delivery of our skills. We learn what the customer wants or how to manage unforeseen situations that might sometimes arise.

This wisdom is not formally taught to us. It is slowly acquired as a result of our myriad experiences. Sometimes it is received via comments from a mentor or supervisor (see Chapter Six). Sometimes it occurs as a result of a setback. At other times, we usefully integrate our wisdom from life in general to the specific demands of our work.

However it happens, we certainly become wiser as a result of our experiences in an employment role and we become more effective as a result. Real estate agents will talk about 'location, location, location', while retailers will say 'the customer is always right'. Plumbers will wisely recount that 'water always flows downhill'. We usually know all this anyway, but it requires a particular skill to blend such commonsense maxims with formal knowledge in a way that gives greater authenticity to one's ability in the role.

If we were able to choose between two midwives, equally well trained, to deliver our baby, we would probably opt for the more experienced practitioner. We will make this decision on the basis of her practical wisdom around childbirth. She will exude commonsense and she will say things like 'work *with* your baby, not against it'. We will be re-assured that she's been here before and that she can apply general principles of care gleaned from her years of experience.

Having said that, it may well be that the older midwife seems too set in her ways and we opt instead for the younger graduate who seems to have her 'feet on the ground', or her 'head set firmly on her shoulders'. Practical commonsense, often gained through a combination of other life experiences, sometimes outweighs the number of years in the job. We might say that a youthful practitioner shows a 'wisdom beyond their years'.

A very practical, sensible friend of mine was a doctor's daughter. As a young girl she often found herself answering the phone and needing to be a calming voice when taking messages. She later claimed that her childhood telephone experiences put her in very good stead for anything that adult life could throw at her. She quickly developed a very wise head on her young shoulders and became a veritable fountain of wisdom, especially around threatened miscarriages! She spoke calmly to women using practical commonsense, often basing her advice on her rapidly accumulating experience. She learned a wise 'bedside manner', and became a very safe pair of hands in a crisis! To this day she continues to serve as a valued confidante for many of her friends in challenging times. Her wisdom was born of a specific skill set at a tender age, but later generalised wonderfully to life and all of its glorious complications.

More recently, a client of mine was describing her work as a shoe salesperson in a large department store. She took pride in her knowledge and could talk endlessly about the range of products that she stocked. She had thousands of rather tedious anecdotes to share about her work experiences. As she spoke, she didn't quite manage to capture or transmit a sense of accumulated wisdom. All the factual information that she could share about shoes did little to inspire me as the listener. Quite frankly, it was boring. But when I asked her, 'What is the key message that you need to share with women to help them choose a pair of shoes?', the tone of the conversation changed. Her reply exuded wisdom. 'Women need to know the difference between fashion and style,' she said. 'Fashion will come and go, but style lasts for ever. They need to find the style that suits them.'

Now this may be old news to those in the fashion industry, but for me, it was a wonderful insight. I was left pondering how my own style might be defined, and how it might better inform my decisions on future shopping expeditions.

It was the power of the second question that lifted the conversation to an altogether more thoughtful level.

_____

Applying Dr Foster's Good Question to your job

Write down your profession or job below:

_____

_____

_____

My role/responsibility is:

_____

_____

_____

_____

Now imagine Dr Foster coming into your workplace and asking politely about your work. And then imagine him asking a more focused version of his incisive second question: _Over all of the time that you've been doing your job, what has it taught you?_

I've learned that: _____

_____

_____

_____

_____

These have been the key insights from my career so far:_____

_____

_____

_____

Key mentors in your working life

Our professional or technical competence is not only based upon our formal training. Apart from our formal education, we have all been informally mentored by lecturers and by supervisors throughout our working life. We can all remember individuals who at various times have given us enormous support and encouragement in our work. We might describe them as inspirational role models.

They have given us practical, commonsense advice and they have modelled how to carry out the job effectively. We have watched them handle difficult situations, and we will have learned simply by working alongside them. But also during the quieter moments, they will have shared some key learnings from their own experiences. Our mentors are a rich source of received wisdom.

_____

Key mentors in my working life

In the left-hand column, write down the names of three people who have been significant influences in your career. They could be lecturers, supervisors, visiting experts or colleagues.

In the right-hand column, write down their single most important message to you. If they could say one thing about the type of work that you do, what would it be?

Name of your mentor	Their key message about the work that you do

And if you could integrate their wisdom into a paramount insight about working well, what would it be? _____

_____

_____

_____

Useful work anecdotes

As we look back over our careers, we can often recall specific incidents that provided great learning opportunities for us. They may be humorous, dramatic or thought-provoking. They are the work stories that we often find ourselves recounting to others as anecdotes. They remain significant to us partly because they carry a generally useful message that we wish to endorse.

Learning from workplace anecdotes

Think back to the stories about your work that you most often recount. They could be disaster stories or they could be funny situations that arise. Describe them briefly in the left-hand column and then stop to consider what the key lesson to the story might be.

My best workplace stories	The key lessons to be learned

Workplace change

So far we have looked at the value of significant stories that we might randomly recall from our career. These contain messages that are familiar to us, and that we recount as fond affirmations of workplace truths.

However, if we now take a little more time to reflect more carefully about the distinct phases of our careers, especially the transition points that have occurred, we will inevitably unearth more specific workplace wisdom. We can learn a great deal about ourselves through workplace change, and by capturing these lessons, even retrospectively, we move forward with a greater clarity about ourselves and the work that we do.

Snippets of wisdom

During my regular, somewhat vacuous conversations with my hairdresser, Sonia, she asked me about my book.

'It's about finding your own wisdom through reflecting on your life so far,' I said. 'For example, when you think back over the changes in your career as a hairdresser, what have been the key changes for you, and what did you learn from them?'

Sonia paused for a moment, cocked her head to one side in that thoughtful little way that hairdressers do, and then replied, 'I suppose when I bought into the business as a partner I suddenly stopped being so accommodating. Previously I'd bend over backwards to fit people in, but business just doesn't work like that. People have to realise that it breaks both ways … people have to learn to fit in with you.'

And just as I smiled at my ability to extract this wise observation from her, Sonia added, 'Also, when my first baby was born, I think that I learned to keep much better boundaries around my conversations with clients. It felt so much more professional to keep a clearer distinction between my work and my personal life.'

Sonia had suddenly become a mine of thoughtful ruminations about her career as a hairdresser. She had experienced and shared two simple 'aha' moments with me. We'd shifted from an idle conversation about holidays and movie stars to talking instead at a conceptual level. It gave us both something to ponder upon later.

Sadly, the shift to big-picture thinking was not sustainable. The nature of both of our personalities meant that we regressed fairly quickly to trading simple Hollywood gossip again.

Whenever changes occur in our life, it is always good to ask ourselves how we have been affected by them. We should actively look for the impact on us and interpret it as a positive change to our character. We may find that we are tougher. Or that we are more sensitive. Or more cautious. Or more resilient.

We can always learn from changes at work and we are usually wiser for the experience. It can make us stronger.

Learning from career transitions

Write down the key phases of your working life to date. You can define these as you like, either referencing different roles, organisations, promotions or bosses. You will know when the key changes occurred for you. Then write down your key workplace learning against each phase. What was the wisdom that you acquired during that phase of your working life?

The key phases of my work life so far	My key learnings from this period

Leadership at work — wisdom from the top

Being *wise* is a fundamental pre-requisite for effective leadership. We expect our leaders to be experienced and to carry a great deal of wisdom as a result. Often we look to them for a reassuring manner in a crisis, trusting in their depth of character. We need them to know themselves well and to know where they are going. We need to trust them, and if we do, then we will follow.

Effective leaders must radiate their values. They do not need to be charismatic, but they do need to quietly broadcast what they stand for. First and foremost, we need to know them for who they are. Simply waving around a fancy vision or a clever strategic plan will never engage potential followers. We need to engage with people's heads *and* their hearts. Leaders cannot expect to take people with them unless they have previously established a connection with their team.

This connection comes through leaders being transparent, visible and clear about who they are as a person. I always make two suggestions to people in a leadership role, whether they are middle managers, chief executives or team leaders. They need to *broadcast* what they are all about.

Firstly, you should share *a leisure interest* or a piece of personal information about yourself that enshrines the values that you wish to promote. If you love jazz, that suggests a creative edge. If you love yacht racing, that suggests a competitive streak.

By leaking a snippet of information about yourself, you will effectively be controlling your image and the chosen interest will promote the values that you espouse. Your team members will ask you about it, will share similar interests and will affirm a similar world view.

Secondly, you should reference *a period in your life* when you were working in accordance with your values. It could have been when you were playing competitive sport, or when you lived on a commune and rode a horse to work. The anecdotes from that period will inevitably reflect your values and the kind of person that you are.

By all means tell staff that you travelled widely in your youth throughout the Third World. But don't tell them that you spent time in jail for inadvertently receiving stolen goods! The inherent message about your values is then just all wrong!

The values of a leader should align perfectly with the values of an organisational culture. Leaders should be aspirational role models for the team.

Leadership applies to us all. We all have our part to play in inspiring and mentoring our colleagues. There will be times when we have to step up and respond to the challenge of a difficult situation or when we need to be authoritative and wise.

Operational leadership requires us to be pragmatic and grounded, while strategic leadership at the top requires us to lift up to a more visionary level. Strategic questions are usually second questions by nature, while operational questions are more likely to be factual in style. The higher we go, the wider is the lens required for us to view the world.

Every member of a team or work group will have their own contribution to make to the leadership team at the appropriate level. By drawing on their personal experience, they offer their unique perspective on the situation, and creative, inspirational insight can come from any team member.

Six effective leadership styles

Daniel Goleman, in his well-known article 'Leadership that gets results' defines six distinct leadership styles. Each has its place and each provides unique strengths. The key message is that it is important not to focus simply on one's own particular style.

1. Coercive leaders drive their staff forwards by demanding compliance. They need their staff to obey unquestioningly and do not value dialogue. This is the style that is prevalent in hierarchical organisations, such as the military or emergency services. Being recognised as *wise* does not play a great part in this style of leadership. There is an implicit assumption that those in authority should simply be obeyed.

2. Authoritative leaders exude an aura of competence based on their knowledge and experience. We follow them because they are more qualified and better informed. Their wisdom is based on their experience. Their style radiates self-assurance.

3. Pace-setting leaders will lead by example, working long hours and modelling high standards for their team. They expect excellence. There is a huge danger of burnout with this unsustainable style of leadership. There is not a huge premium placed on wisdom. It is mostly a matter of being extremely competent and leading by example.

4. Democratic leadership promotes *buy in* from all team members. Attention is paid to the process of shared decision making, such that everyone feels part of any decision that is made. The leader engages with their team as part of their team. They build consensus through participation. They are not necessarily wise about the content of the job, but they are often wise about process and managing people.

5. Affiliative leaders place a strong emphasis on the relationship with each member. It is all about *us* and *we*. There is a strong heart connect between team members and values such as loyalty and commitment predominate. Staff will follow because they believe in their leader and the leader's values. Affiliative leaders often get more out of their teams than is logical for them to give. They will work late, stay committed, and take a lower wage if it leads to success for the team. The wisdom of an affiliative leader is best described as *empathic wisdom,* as shown by an effective yet caring parent.

6. Coaching leadership is the closest we come to a *wise* leadership as defined in this book. Coaching leaders will invest in their team and mentor them. They are keen to get the best out of team members by taking the time to encourage growth. Their focus is not so much on the demands of the task in hand, but how their team can learn most from the experience and be better equipped in the future. They will always ask good questions that elicit awareness in others.

Leadership at work is not a one-size-fits-all affair. The different leadership styles require us to be wise in different ways and at different times. Leadership and wisdom are inextricably linked. The wisest leaders are also highly skilled in personal reflection where they value the opportunity to ask challenging questions of themselves.

My leadership style

When you are obliged to pick up a responsibility for managing others at work, whether as a CEO or as a labourer getting his team to shovel dirt, consider the following questions:

- What is your typical leadership style? _____

  _____

  _____

- What are the strengths of this style? _____

  _____

  _____

- What is your least preferred style? _____

  _____

- How could you develop this style? _____

  _____

  _____

- What added advantages would this bring to your work? _____

  _____

  _____

  _____

_____

Summary

In this chapter we have looked at the role of wisdom at work. We have seen how the insights gained through our *practical experience* will always complement our training qualifications.

We have looked at wisdom received from our *mentors* and the inherently wise messages embedded in the *anecdotes* that we share. We have looked at the wisdom that we have gained at *different stages* of our careers, and noted the lessons learned from each *career transition*.

Finally, we have looked at the *wisdom of leadership* and have seen how the different leadership styles incorporate varying shades of wisdom.

It is important to recognise and nurture the development of a *wise persona* at work. A workplace setting is the ideal forum for our personal wisdom to be acknowledged and truly valued. Wisdom at work is sought after, appreciated and highly valued by others. If we've got it, then we should surely share it.

Chapter Twelve

WHEN WISDOM GOES WRONG

Sometimes, people derive unhelpful or distorted insights from their life experiences. They carry a kind of *flawed wisdom* that hinders their effectiveness in life. They have a problem with the *content* of their thoughts and beliefs, which subsequently holds them back.

For others the problem concerns a failure to *communicate* their wisdom effectively. They fail to influence the thinking of others in positive ways. It is more a problem of *style*. Their timing is poor, they broadcast too much and they make excessive use of personal anecdote. Sometimes, perhaps not surprisingly, expressed wisdom can be extremely boring and tedious for others.

Faulty wisdom — problems with content

The subjective nature of wisdom means that often it can trip us up. Sometimes our life experiences lead us to make assumptions about the world that are at best unhelpful and at worst simply wrong.

We might decide that we are unworthy or unlucky. Or that we cannot trust the world to be safe. We may feel unlovable or that we will always be abandoned by those whom we love. We draw up generic conclusions about life, based on our experiences, and then view everything through this dysfunctional lens. Our wisdom about the world is faulty, and it holds us back.

For therapists, faulty wisdom is a major focus of their work. Exploring and re-formulating faulty assumptions made by a client is the key theme to any therapeutic conversation. Dysfunctional assumptions are identified and challenged, allowing for healthier, more adaptive 'truths' to be established. This becomes the new wisdom for the client and it often comes to them in a blinding 'aha'.

At other times, a client may come along for weeks and weeks, struggling to describe their problems or to articulate the key issue. Therapeutic patience is required here, as the client slowly works towards the realisation of what faulty assumptions and beliefs underpin their presenting problem. As new insights are slowly gained, there follows a slow but inevitable dawning of a new world view. The client learns a more empowering and affirming view of the world. Therapist and client together chip away at long-held and long-cherished dysfunctional beliefs, and a new door slowly opens — a weight has been lifted.

Regardless of the speed of therapy, the basis for any therapeutic change is for the therapist to ask good second questions that challenge the dysfunctional wisdom. Examples might be:

- Of all the things that we've spoken about so far, what is the most problematic thinking pattern that you notice?

- If you could live in a perfect world, what would be different for you?

- Of all the things that you hear yourself saying, what is holding you back the most?

After the inevitable pause the client will reply, and in doing so, they will look beyond the constraints of their problem-oriented world view. They will think more expansively and their subsequent insights will allow them to install a more constructive perspective on their world. Examples might be:

- I'm not stuck, I have options!

- The past is behind me, I should let it go. I now need to be focusing on the future.

- It's not up to others to decide, it's up to me to choose what happens next!

- I just need to change the way I look at the world.

All of these sudden realisations might seem obvious to a detached observer, but to the client, the revelation blows away a long-standing, deeply entrenched counter view. The pre-existing concept of being stuck, for example, has probably been unhelpful for many years, but it seemed so true to the client that, over time, it became a fact.

The usual experience of a therapeutic 'aha' moment provides for personal empowerment and for the adoption of a new maxim. The 'aha' moments invariably occur in response to a specific second question from the therapist. By *lifting up* from an endless review of their problematic world, or *stepping back* from life, or by *digging deeper* into subconscious layers of thought, the client has been given the opportunity to think more expansively.

The power of a second question is at its greatest when precipitating a therapeutic 'aha' moment. The axis shifts imperceptibly at first, then suddenly tips from negative to positive self-talk. The client moves from entrenched maladaptive habits to more adaptive routines. They move from pessimism to optimism. They are dramatically freed up to change. Challenging the validity of maladaptive or faulty wisdom is the essence of good therapy. Good second questions can deliver fantastic outcomes.

Recognising and challenging *faulty wisdom* in ourselves, or ideas that are not helpful to us, is an important part of knowing oneself. We are learning to be wise about ourselves in a different way. We can see our failings and our flaws. We can re-define the picture, and as a result we can take greater control of our lives.

Failure to communicate wisdom — problems of style

One of the great tragedies of life is that, as we grow older, our wisdom somehow becomes marginalised and we seem to lose our relevance. Grumpy old men and opinionated housewives drift off towards the shadowy corners of life, their sage advice no longer valued or sought after by the young. The elderly tend to talk excessively and tediously about the good old days and they complain vehemently in response to innovation and change. They wear their wisdom like they wear their clothes — limp, shabby and drab.

Despite the enduring relevance of their wisdom, the elderly and the arrogant often lose the ability to broadcast their contributions effectively. All too often, they simply give advice, express negative opinions, and become judgmental about the world around them.

There is nothing worse than those boring old characters in the corner of the staff room, or propping up the bar, who think that they know it all. They have lost the art of using good questions to tease out wisdom from others.

They are no longer mentoring, they are simply lecturing from a haughty position. Their wise counsel no longer hits the mark, and they start squandering the opportunities that still exist for them to influence the world around them.

A similar issue can happen to experienced therapists or teachers who increasingly rely on their experience and collection of tried and true anecdotes to make a point. They become complacent, and their stories slowly lose their impact and relevance. The world is always changing and the lessons drawn from the past can become tiresome, even if there are useful parallels to be drawn.

Two particularly common pitfalls (misreading your audience and excessively rigid wisdom) are considered below.

Misreading your audience

We have already identified two key areas where communication problems can arise for the wise. Firstly, we have seen that excessive broadcasting of personal anecdote and metaphor can be tiresome. Secondly, we have seen that expressed and valued personal anecdotes may not resonate with the other person.

It is important to remember that it is far more effective to *elicit* wisdom in others than it is to *offer* it. In the end, it's all about asking those good second questions.

For some people, conceptual thinking is a bore and takes them to a place that they'd rather not go. For them, wisdom is something that is only of interest to others. It should be acknowledged that the diffuse nature of the *world of insight* is not for everyone and many wise evangelical conversations have fallen on deaf ears due simply to a lack of interest.

I don't want to have insights!

Peter, a retired engineer, maths teacher and a lifelong contentious friend, asked me what my new book was going to be about. I explained about second questions and their power to elicit insights. His reply took me aback!

I don't want to have insights. Second questions sound arrogant. I'm happy just to live in a world of facts and information. Why should I care about becoming wise? It's nice just seeing the world as it is and enjoying the experience. I don't want to think big!

Peter probably speaks for many people. The idea of knowing yourself better and seeing the world conceptually may seem to be rather elitist, especially if someone else is suggesting that it's good for you. Like Peter, many people are content to simply wander through life without taking the time to reflect, without lifting up from the daily routines and without seeing a bigger picture.

For most of us it is simply that our lives are too busy or that we are too caught up in facts and figures to stop and find the time to know ourselves, who we are, and what we stand for. Making time for structured reflection is one of the greatest gifts that we can give ourselves. It's easy and it's free. But it's also discretionary!

There is a place in the world for intuitive types, for concrete thinkers and for people who enjoy stepwise deductive reasoning. Many of life's great pleasures derive from simple activities and skills based on practical knowledge. However, second questions provide a gateway to a much wider world, where an array of conceptual delights and insights can occur. In many ways, it's generally a more thoughtful and satisfying pleasure to put two and two together, and make far more than four!

However, when we become over-enthusiastic about new ideas or become overly driven to share our insights with the rest of the world, we are in danger of alienating everyone from the message. We should always make sure that people want to operate on a higher conceptual level before we rush in with the new ideas. Sometimes, the gates can only be opened so far. People have to *want* to step through to experience the wisdom of the wider world.

Excessively rigid wisdom

Another sobering aspect to the concept of wisdom is the familiar saying that 'there's no fool like an old fool'. This phrase, so often used, contains good advice about how age can lead us to a cast-iron sense of certainty that we are 'right' or that we can trust our judgments over and above what is prudent.

Old fools don't see that what has applied for them in the past may no longer apply in the present, or that times have changed. They have become set in their ways and set in their beliefs. Rather than having minds that are open to learning about the world, their rigidity means that they are actually closed.

Old fools appear arrogant and they broadcast rather than listen. They have forgotten that the mark of true wisdom is to listen with genuine curiosity before asking questions. Curiosity requires us to stay innovative and flexible in our interactions with the world.

Summary

In this chapter we have briefly reviewed how wisdom can go wrong.

Firstly, we have seen how dysfunctional thinking can lead to *faulty wisdom* about the world. If left unchallenged, it can lead us into a seriously flawed world view.

Secondly, we have noted that wisdom often fails to be *communicated effectively*. A tired, rigid and boorish approach will leave others cold. It also keeps the broadcaster in an increasingly isolated place; they are surrounded by the fixed ideas that they have espoused, and have inadvertently built a wall around themselves.

There is nothing quite so sad as a wise individual sitting alone like a fool on a hill. The sun will surely go down on them, and their valued wisdom will inevitably be lost as a consequence.

Chapter Thirteen

PULLING IT ALL TOGETHER

It is now time to pull together the wisdom that we have discovered into a coherent summary. For some it will be enough to simply sit back and draw up a summary paragraph about themselves — rather like a personal summary we may write about ourselves on the home page of a website or on a Facebook page. Or the paragraph that we are required to write about our personal qualities on a CV. For others it may be enough simply to reflect upon some of the broader questions that were asked. You might ask yourself:

- What will my headstone say? How will my epitaph read?
- What are the deepest values that I carry and the most inspirational personal qualities that I admire?
- What will my legacy be?
- What would be the title to the story of my life?

Each one of these questions is huge and can only be answered after a period of focused self-reflection.

Having worked through the exercises listed in the book, you will feel much better equipped to answer the three big questions: *Who am I? What have I learned?* and *What do I stand for?*

When Dr Foster drifted into my life all those years ago, he asked me a simple question. He asked me what I had learned in my life so far. And I couldn't answer him. But in that moment I had a blinding insight about what was lacking in my life and also in the life of most people around me.

We simply don't ask ourselves the bigger questions these days. We don't celebrate the wisdom gained through our personal life experiences and we don't pause often enough to reflect on what we have learned and what we feel is important.

For many of you, the experience of reading this book will undoubtedly provide several 'Dr Foster' moments. The book will have asked questions to which you have no idea what your answer might be. You simply hadn't ever stopped to consider what you really think about the important stuff, and no one had ever bothered to ask you. You certainly hadn't stopped to ask yourself.

The tragedy of our lives is that we don't stop to reflect. We don't pause and celebrate what we have learned or achieved. We have wonderful moments of blinding insight, but then let them slip away. We stay so grounded in the business of living our daily lives that we don't lift our heads up to marvel at the bigger picture.

When choosing a seat on a plane, we might be asked whether we prefer a window or an aisle seat. The aisle seat offers us a practical connection to the exit, to the overhead lockers, to the flight attendants trolley and to the toilets. Conversely, the window seat offers us an opportunity to gaze out across the world. To marvel at the vastness of the landscape and to reflect upon the wonderful experience of being alive.

This book is all about choosing the window seat. To deliberately create occasions in your everyday life where you set up the scene for expansive thought. To find opportunities to reflect and to think about the bigger picture.

When we sit in the darkness of a cinema or in the stillness of a church, or when we sit as part of a spellbound audience at a concert, we feel transformed. We become connected with something bigger than the immediate present. We hear simple truths broadcast that seem to speak perfectly for us about life, the universe and just about everything else.

The hook lines in the choruses of our favourite pop songs carry so much meaning for us. They become ingrained in our psyche. We recognise the melodies immediately. We hum the tunes without realising what we are doing.

Similarly, we may often reference passages from our favourite books or couplets from a poem or nursery rhyme. We may find ourselves describing a scene from a movie in order to convey a powerful message about life or relationships. We are drawn to tragedy, to humour and sometimes to farce.

Our ears pick up when we hear a reference to people that we admire. We celebrate their legacy and the inherent values shown by our role models from the past. These things can move us deeply at an emotional level and they connect us to their wisdom.

Wisdom is not something that we *do*. It is something that we *are*. Wise people provide anchors or reference points for those around them. They do not need to prove that they are wise; we just know that it is an inherent state of being. Wise individuals carry their wisdom calmly and with self-assuredness. People seek them out, not necessarily for advice but as a sounding board for their own ideas. Wise people trade in wise thoughts. They offer wisdom and they elicit wisdom.

Wisdom tends to come with age and experience. We should embrace it. We should learn to value the lines on our face, and the twists and the turns that our life has taken. We need to age with grace and with dignity, and to be prepared to step up to leadership roles and responsibilities with confidence. We need to be kind, wise and knowledgeable, radiating our values clearly and exuding a sense of calm self-assurance. We should graciously accept the role of being sought out by family and friends for our ideas.

Years ago I attended a concert by Johnny Dankworth and Cleo Laine in Dunedin's Regent Theatre in New Zealand. I went out of curiosity to see these legendary husband-and-wife jazz musicians on their final world tour. It was a miserable night in the middle of the week at the bottom of the world. The rain lashed relentlessly down on the theatre roof. I found myself sitting in a sea of soaking wet grey hair and heavy, saturated overcoats.

The lights dimmed and the curtains drew back. Johnny Dankworth stepped out onto the stage, neatly dressed in a smart suit. As the applause faded, he gestured simply with his hands to the audience before speaking warmly from the stage.

> *Ladies and Gentlemen. I cannot tell you how honoured we are that you have chosen to come out on such a dreadful night to see us perform. We are truly humbled, and I can guarantee that we will do our very, very best to repay your faith in us.*

There was uproar in the house! Before the concert had even begun we knew that we were in the presence of a very special man.

I was absolutely blown away by the humility and respect that was inherent in his opening words. His warmth, integrity and self-assurance as a person just shone through his remarks. He knew his stuff. He was wise. And he was a man who knew how he wanted to be.

I later contrasted the humility and kindness of Johnny Dankworth's opening remarks with other, younger, more impulsive musicians that I had seen on that very same stage. They tended to strut and to posture. They thought that they knew it all. They were out to prove that they were the best. They were technically superb, but somehow they lacked 'presence'. They were self-assured, but they did not seem wise.

As we move through life we will inevitably come across and notice wise people. We will see inspirational politicians or spiritual leaders conducting media interviews. We will also meet experienced professionals who impress us with their confident, self-assured interpersonal style. We might remember doctors, midwives and funeral directors who calmly guided us through difficult times in our lives.

We may also read about successful business entrepreneurs who share the simple rules that helped them to get ahead in life. They will all describe simple insights that provide the guiding principles for the decisions that they made in their careers, and these insights often become repeated endlessly as mottos or mantras. The famous will readily share and promote one or two values that they hold as the key to their success.

They will all seem to *know* a great deal, but some of them will carry an additional aura of *wisdom*. They will be trading in simple truths; they will be humble; and they will be drawing on their personal experience.

Anyone who has cause to reflect on their good luck, their bad luck or even their indifferent luck will benefit from stopping to think. By pausing to reflect, they will inevitably gain insights into their life and they will be wiser for having made the effort.

From time to time we will also come across people who have experienced personal trauma or who have lost loved ones. It is a natural part of life. We might also find ourselves talking to people who have recently cheated death or to people who are facing death. Invariably, they will all be profoundly lost in a search for meaning. They have seen beyond the framework of their daily routines and simple assumptions, and the bigger questions will inevitably arise.

Conversely we may meet people who have recently found love or who are celebrating the birth of their child. They are glowing in response to their experience and they, too, find themselves floating in a sea of wondrous questions and stunning insights about what life is all about. Circumstance has lifted them out of the mundane and into the world of big-picture thinking.

These differing events in our lives, often unscripted and unexpected, provide opportunities for us all to pause and reflect. In these moments of overwhelming and often profoundly confusing emotions, we have the opportunity to learn so much about ourselves. And the best way to gain clarity from confusion is by asking good questions. This is the way that we make sense of our lives.

At the end of the day becoming wiser is very simple. It all comes back to Dr Foster's Good Question or any variant of it that you choose to ask of yourself. Second questions are powerful tools. They lift you up to see the bigger picture. They force you to stop, to take a breath, and to touch base with a broader overview of the world. You learn to see your place in the wider frame.

Second questions are fun, life-affirming, and thought-provoking challenges. They elicit delightful insights about life, and they create powerful understandings of who you really are.

Second questions provide us with a gateway to wisdom. They invite blue-sky thinking and panoramic views. And in response to the invitation, we can all feel more expansive and free, at the same time connecting more authentically with who we are.

Big-picture thinking gives life a greater sense of purpose and fulfilment. Over time, the search for meaning becomes increasingly compelling as we accumulate our collection of insights. By persevering in our search for personal wisdom, and by making dedicated time for it, we will feel increasingly satisfied and contented in our lives.

And when awkward curmudgeons like Dr Foster come calling again, we will be so much better equipped to deal with their pesky questions. We shall be truly wise!

BIBLIOGRAPHY

Ehrmann, Max (1927), *Desiderata*

George, Bill (2007), *True North: Discover your authentic leadership style,* Wiley, San Fransisco, CA.

Gibran, Khalil (1923), *The Prophet.*

Goleman, Daniel (2000), 'Leadership that gets results', *Harvard Business Review.*

Goleman, Daniel (2011), *The Brain and Emotional Intelligence: New insights,* More Than Sound, LLC Northampton, MA (e-book).

Harris, Russ (2009), *ACT Made Simple: An easy to read primer on Acceptance and Commitment Therapy*, New Harbinger Publications, Oakland, CA.

Kipling, Rudyard (1910), *If,* first published in *Rewards and Fairies,* Macmillan and Co. Ltd, London.

Kolb, D. (1984), *Experiential Learning: Experience as the source of learning and development*, Prentice Hall, Englewood Cliffs, NJ.

Luft, J. & Ingham, H. (1955), 'The Johari Window, a graphic model of interpersonal awareness', *Proceedings of the western training laboratory in group development,* Los Angeles, UCLA.

Neibuhr, Reinhold (1943), *The Serenity Prayer*

Oxford Dictionary of Quotations, The (2009), Oxford University Press, Oxford, UK.

INDEX

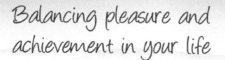

Balancing pleasure and
achievement in your life

When
HAPPINESS
IS NOT
ENOUGH

CHRIS SKELLETT

An extract from *When Happiness is Not Enough*,
also by Chris Skellett, and available from:
www.exislepublishing.com
ISBN 978 1 921497 17 9

Chapter One
AN INTRODUCTION TO THE PLEASURE/ACHIEVEMENT PRINCIPLE

Everybody wants to be happy. We all know when we're happy and when we're sad, and our life is full of decisions made in our search for happiness. We make these decisions from moment to moment and from year to year. And usually, we tend to base our decisions on a generalised theme or preference. For example, we might prefer excitement to comfort, or change rather than stability. These trends and preferences are many and varied, and they can all play out in different ways.

But of all the different factors that drive our decisions and shape our behaviour, there is one simple truth that underpins our complex lives more than any other. Specifically, we need to ensure that in all aspects of our lives, we maintain a healthy balance between *the drive for pleasure* and the *drive for satisfaction through achievement*. Happiness is to be found by combining them both.

The concepts sound so similar, and both feel good, but a closer analysis shows that they are two very different emotions. We tend to use the words 'pleasure' and 'satisfaction' interchangeably, and we do not take due care in distinguishing between the two. 'It gives me great pleasure …' and 'I take great satisfaction …' are two phrases that sound very much the same. But by failing to discriminate, we fail to balance the two concepts and, as a result, we fail in our efforts to live a balanced and fulfilling life.

The secret to living an enjoyable, rewarding life is to balance pleasure and achievement, and to be mindful of the relative importance of these two key drivers.

> The Pleasure/Achievement Principle can be defined thus:
> *In order to live a fulfilling life, we must strike a considered balance between pleasure and achievement.*

Essentially, we need to become more aware of whether we tend to seek pleasure in our lives, or whether we instead strive to experience satisfaction through achieving personal goals. In order to develop our awareness of this issue, we will need to look at the two key concepts in a little more detail.

Pleasure

Pleasure is based on short-term gratification. It's fun, it's indulgent, and it's the basis of humour, enjoyment and a sense of contentment. With pleasure, we live in the moment. We feel alive and we love the sensual delights that are on offer. We relax, we feel comfortable, and we soak up life to the full. Our base instincts are to seek pleasure, and for many, experiencing pleasure is the ultimate goal of a life well lived! We value and define our happiness in this way. *We remember the fun that we've had.*

When we are pleasure focused, life is to be savoured; it is to be appreciated for the way that it is. We are happy to simply enjoy. We feel relaxed, and we look back on a day of pleasurable experiences. *Our smiles are happy smiles.*

Satisfaction

Satisfaction is different. It is based on the achievement of personal goals. We set goals, we achieve them, and we feel satisfied as a result. Satisfaction is usually achieved by overriding the short-term pain and discomfort of action in pursuit of a chosen goal. We dig deep and admire our strength and our energy. We value motivation, drive and ambition. We climb mountains; we win gold. *We remember the things that we've achieved.*

When we are achievement focused, there are always improvements to be made, things to learn and opportunities to explore. We make lists, we work hard, and by the end of the day we are tired. We look back at what we have achieved. *Our smiles are satisfied smiles.*

•

While pleasure tends to be a transient experience, feelings of satisfaction are usually longer lasting. Some of us look for what there is to be enjoyed in the present, right now. Others look ahead to what could be achieved in the future, and they also look back to remember what has been achieved in the past. They value outcomes that occur over time.

Pleasure, achievement and lifestyle problems

When a pleasure focus becomes excessive, we can find ourselves drifting into a variety of unhealthy lifestyles. Pleasurable indulgence can lead to laziness, depressive lethargy, or self-control issues. We show an excess of what psychologists call *consummatory behaviours,* where we 'consume' opportunities for pleasure. We seek comfort and contentment in our lives. We often become complacent with ourselves, and our physical health suffers.

When an achievement focus becomes excessive, however, different problems emerge. The drive to achieve can result in stress, anxiety and a generalised inability to relax or feel good about ourselves. We live *appetitively*, where we are 'hungry' and constantly needing to satisfy our 'appetite' for more. We often carry a generalised restlessness in our daily lives. We are always looking ahead and trying to improve. There is a continual urge to effect change. Life is always full of possibilities, but it can become a tiring theme both for ourselves and for those around us.

Clearly, a number of clinical problems can arise if there is a significant imbalance between pleasure and achievement in our lives.

An excessive focus on pleasure will lead to a certain class of lifestyle problems. Most self-control issues for individuals — such as over-eating, alcohol or substance abuse and gambling — are based on an excessive focus on short-term pleasure. We become over-indulgent.

To counter this, self-control programs will set clear goals for individuals to achieve. We are encouraged to lose weight, to save money or to give up smoking. We keep records and we monitor progress. And when we achieve our goals, we feel satisfied. By exercising self-control, we are essentially re-focusing on experiencing a sense of 'satisfaction' in the longer term, instead of choosing more 'pleasurable' experiences in the shorter term.

Similarly, most programs that promote physical fitness and health will encourage us to make consistent lifestyle decisions based on achievement. These are always referenced towards the achievement of future, satisfying goals, rather than the enjoyment or pleasure of the present moment. In other words, we have to suspend current pleasure in order to achieve greater satisfaction in the future.

We often hear people saying, 'I don't like going to the gym.' But few people ever go to the gym because they enjoy it, or because they find it 'pleasurable'. Instead, they go to 'achieve' fitness and muscle tone. It's hard work. But like work, the key driver for them is the satisfaction experienced at the end of the session. If we happen to enjoy it too, that's great, but it's not the key driver. For most of us, going to the gym is an ultimately satisfying activity if the goals are achieved. But it is rarely a pleasurable activity while you're actually there!

An excessive focus on achievement will create a different class of psychological problems for an individual. There will be an over-emphasis on achieving certain goals or standards. Stress, burnout and obsessive problems all derive from an overvalued desire to achieve. People display an unrelenting drive to improve or to make changes. They seem restless and strive for a satisfaction that is rarely attained. They are so pressured and busy that their relationships suffer. For these people, achievement must be balanced with a greater degree of pleasure in their lives. Essentially, these folk need to learn to stop and 'smell the roses'.

Emotions and the Pleasure/Achievement Principle

Our mood is also determined by the complex interplay between pleasure and achievement. When we feel bored or depressed, we will often eat chocolate, lie in bed and generally indulge ourselves. We feel sad. We want to feel happy. We attempt to compensate for our sadness by treating ourselves to some pleasure. We focus on this form of happiness and try to cheer ourselves up with a good time. But these pleasure-oriented actions serve to give only short-term respite from sadness before we sink back and feel even worse than before.

In contrast to treating ourselves with pleasurable experiences when we feel depressed, we need instead to seek a deeper sense of happiness through satisfaction. The more lasting pathway out of depression is to set simple goals, to establish a sense of purpose, and to aim for a more enduring sense of satisfaction. By taking small, tangible steps towards a more active lifestyle, we achieve a steady accumulation of satisfying experiences. As a result, the passive sense of helplessness that typically characterises a depressive mindset slowly dissipates. In this way, it turns out that seeking satisfaction is the primary antidote to depression, not indulging in gratuitous pleasure.

Paradoxically, an excessive indulgence in pleasure will eventually leave us feeling empty and flat. Life's 'endless party' ceases to be fun and life can seem superficial. There is no momentum, no drive and no sense of fulfilment. We become dissatisfied. We lack motivation or ambition, and ultimately, life can feel pointless.

In Chapter Ten, we will briefly review a range of clinical issues that can arise in everyday life, and that can be usefully considered from a pleasure/achievement perspective.

Ageing with style and purpose

The relevance of pleasure and satisfaction often varies at different stages of our lives. Different generations face different challenges, and common problems and tensions will arise.

Teenagers and students, for example, face the constant dilemma of balancing academic achievement with the more seductive pleasures of partying around town. Their lives can often become based on the unrelenting pursuit of social pleasures, at the expense of study and hard work. But then, at the end of the year, life suddenly becomes all about grades again, and priorities need to be hastily reviewed!

Invariably, decisions at this age are finely balanced between the urge to experience pleasure and the need to achieve. But we do not always recognise our own decision-making patterns in this respect. We do not necessarily see that we have choices. As a result, we simply stumble on through life without much pause for thought.

In addition, teenagers' attitudes are also strongly shaped by the opinions and values of those who surround them. The influence and attitudes of their peers and role models are often a huge factor in shaping their lifestyle values. Their heroes are either highly successful achievers in their chosen field, or else they are highly engaging, charismatic personalities who fascinate us because of *who* they are rather than anything they achieve.

At school, did we prioritise homework or TV? Did we spend our free time in the library, or did we goof off to the park?

As students, did we prefer to spend our time in the library or in the pub? Were we more often found sitting at a desk or lying on the couch? Did we tend to go out on the town or did we choose to have an early night instead?

Usually, unless we are particularly careful, it is those invitations to pleasure that drive our decisions during our young adult years!

During *adult life*, we all find ourselves caught up in an achievement-oriented world. Developing careers, raising children and paying off mortgages all become major themes to our lives. Promotions, social status and the acquisition of wealth become more relevant. Often we resent the pressure, but it's all around us. Every day we are either getting a little further ahead or a little further behind.

But later … at the other end of our adult lives, the pleasure/achievement issue swings around again to the other extreme. In *retirement*, the dilemma suddenly becomes one of learning to disengage from a productive life and instead value the opportunity to sit back and enjoy life for what it has to offer. The transition from pleasure to productivity is again reversed, and we learn to value the simple art of enjoyment once more.

Grumpy old men are usually the direct result of a failure to manage this issue. As they age, they can no longer achieve to the same standard. They become frustrated at their inability to perform to the same levels. For them, there is so much to be gained by simply shifting sideways towards a greater pleasure orientation in their lives, and to just enjoy life for what it is.

In summary, we all tend to struggle with finding the right balance for ourselves during life's transitions. In Chapter Four, we shall be reviewing the role of pleasure and achievement during the seven stages of our lives, and we will reflect on our personal journey so far in order to gain useful insights.

EXISLE PUBLISHING — e-newsletter

If you love books as much as we do, why not subscribe
to our weekly e-newsletter?

As a subscriber, you'll receive special offers and discounts,
be the first to hear of our exciting upcoming titles, and
be kept up to date with book tours and author events.
You will also receive unique opportunities exclusive
to subscribers – and much more!

To subscribe in Australia or from any other
country except New Zealand, visit
www.exislepublishing.com.au/newsletter-sign-up

For New Zealand, visit
www.exislepublishing.co.nz/newsletter-subscribe